WORLD IN REBELLION

by

John E. Hunter

MOODY PRESS • CHICAGO

CONTENTS

© 1972 by
THE MOODY BIBLE INSTITUTE
OF CHICAGO

ISBN: 0-8024-9680-6

Printed in the United States of America

FOREWORD

Any book blessed of God must first be born in the heart of a man blessed of God. Such a book is *World in Rebellion*. John Hunter is one of God's chosen prophets. He speaks and writes with the obvious anointing of God's Spirit upon him. It has been my privilege to know him and to experience the warmth and radiance of his dynamic life in Christ and his Spirit-controlled ministry for many years. He can hold an audience of collegians and/or middle-aged listeners spellbound for an hour or more and then send them out to purchase his books for a restatement of what they have just heard.

One of the reasons for John Hunter's mastery over his audience and his readers is his clear grasp of biblical truths. This grows not only out of his diligent study of God's Word but also out of a rich personal experience of knowing the Lord Jesus as the indwelling Christ.

In *World in Rebellion* the author shows that the reason for the rebellious flare-up in today's world is the vigorous anti-God action of Satan, which started with his rebellion against God in heaven and continues on earth. Dr. Hunter exposes the root of the problem that we see today and uses the Bible to show us God's perspective. He interprets Scripture in the light of today's headlines and interprets the headlines in the light of Scripture. God's counterattack in sending Jesus Christ as Saviour brings the reader front and center to the greatest drama of all time—the cross. The author gives a comprehensive view of the whole plan of redemption, making clear the necessity of the blood. He places a wholesome emphasis upon a positive man, in a manner that is theologically clear without being overly precise.

3

To the question, Is continuous victory a possibility for the Christian? John Hunter answers with a resounding yes! He tells how we can become happy, joyful, successful Christians and then follows with a practical chapter on what he considers the most needed teaching in the church today—how to experience God's power in our lives. Then he proceeds to show the reasons for failure to gain victory, as illustrated by Israel and key men of the Bible. Success requires that we actually know Jesus Christ personally. It is not enough to do, act, and talk like a Christian: we must know Christ! Many people fear to take Christ as Lord, although they profess Him as Saviour. John Hunter shows why it is necessary to "seek Me with all your heart" (Jeremiah 29:13) —the whole heart, intellect, emotions and will! Finally, the author takes us by the hand and shows us step by step the way to the joy and peace of victory as believers.

World in Rebellion puts it all together, and for that reason this book could be considered a primer for new Christians. Yet it is more, for it will help many believers to gain new victories as they experience the vital new relationship which is theirs through Jesus Christ.

BILL BRIGHT
Founder and President
Campus Crusade for Christ International

PART I

THE TEACHING OF TRUTH

1

THE CAUSE OF REBELLION

HAVE YOU READ words like these recently?

Mid-East Talks Break Down
Riot Breaks Out in College Campus
Guerrillas Strike Against Government Again
Rebellious Youths Break Up Local Dance
Police Unable to Control Protest Rampage

I'm sure you are tired of opening your paper and seeing such headlines. As I have traveled from country to country in recent months, in Australia, Europe, United States, South America, and up through the countries of the Orient, this has been the regular pattern of newspaper comment. Regardless of language used, the message has been the same, rebellion against authority.

There always has been an undercurrent of dissatisfaction in every country, and certain countries have been noted for their occasional uprises and disturbances. But never has there been such a worldwide bursting forth of seething anger and open defiance. Countries that once looked down from their pinnacles of peace upon the sporadic outbursts of lesser nations have been toppled and humbled into shame as they, too, have been torn with acts of violence.

This rebellion is proving now to be widespread in every area of human relationship. On the international level we see behavior between nations that in previous years would have been classed as war. Attacks made, lives lost, damage

7

done in what can be described only as defiance of agreements once mutually agreed upon.

The national daily life of many countries is being torn by acts of destruction from within. At the city level protests and demonstrations come with bewildering suddenness.

I have never seen such internal strife as is evident now in some leading church denominations, even down to the local churches.

Home life in most of the leading and affluent nations is nothing less than stark tragedy. There seems to be an insidious destruction of national life at home level. Deteriorated husband-wife relationships plus the tangle of parent-children relationships have reduced much of family life to minor warfare or sporadic guerrilla attacks.

These conditions always have existed in a lesser degree, but never before has there been such a worldwide boiling up of near madness in human relations.

The purpose of this book is to trace the source and the cause of all rebellion, using the Bible for reference and instruction. Then we shall see what means God has provided to meet such situations, finding how it is possible to handle the real root area of rebellion—the human heart.

The human heart is the prime source of all such acts, whether international, national, domestic, or personal. "Things" do not move into acts of open defiance; they may be involved, but they never originate the acts. Only the action and response of a human heart can bring about these miserable situations. We say, "Great doors turn on little hinges" and how true! Every calamitous confrontation in human history has swung into being on the hinge of human hearts.

No wonder the Bible says, "The heart is deceitful above all things, and desperately wicked: who can know it?" (Jer 17:9). Incidentally, the word "deceitful" in this verse means crooked or slippery. The words "desperately wicked" mean sick. How true this is, just as we see it around us in the crooked, slippery acts of people who are "sick" to the depths of their beings. And we see this in the sad experiences of our own behavior.

Where did this rebellion first begin? The wildness of today's youth or the planned wickedness of communist intrigue are blamed for many of the disturbing situations in the world today; but they are only symptoms of the disease, not the source of the defiance. It comes as a great surprise to many people to learn that rebellion did not begin in any present-day country or in any nation of past history. It did not find its origin in this world at all. This ugly, worldwide situation began in heaven, within the confines of the glory of God!

This challenges us with immediate questions. Why did this situation develop? Didn't God know? Why did God allow this hideous insurrection? The Bible contains the information to guide us into a better understanding of the subject of rebellion. But we need to realize at the outset that the purpose of the Bible is not to answer the questions of the human heart. The Bible does not tell us what we *want* to know, but what we *need* to know in order to find an answer to our heart's rebellion and to gain peace with God. To all who continue to *demand* answers to their questions, the Bible maintains the silence of God, except to point out that the demanding heart is a further demonstration of rebellion.

Let us turn to the Word of God and find the cause of this world's upsurging defiance. Revelation 20:2 gives four names of the one responsible: "The dragon, that old serpent, which is the Devil, and Satan." He is the one behind the beginning of rebellion and is responsible for seeing it continue and increase.

Now notice something very unusual. Not very long ago, if a Christian speaking to a non-Christian were to mention belief in a personal devil, he would be a cause for ridicule. The unbeliever would laugh openly at his incredulity or else show amazement that he could believe in myths and fairy tales. It was accepted that no intelligent person maintained this old-fashioned idea. Educated people knew better. Belief in Satan belonged to the middle ages of history, or to ignorant pagans living in a backward culture. But have you noticed over the last few years a quiet, unrecognized change of belief?

When I came to the United States four years ago, the new discovery in theological circles was "God is dead." Much comment and controversy was raised as a result. But in the last year the ferment has died down—the "God is dead" theory is dead! Instead, something more fearful has come in—"Satan is alive!"

There is no doubt that the upsurge of the drug culture with its blasting away of time-honored restraints has encouraged open recognition of Satan as a reality. Suddenly the civilized world is alive to the new developments in Satan worship and the host of other demonic institutions. Witchcraft, once hidden because of its unlovely connections, is now a booming movement, in Britain and the United States in particular. Satan is out in the open, vaunting himself with all his pride. Satan is respectable; witches are accepted; involvement with demons is the latest attraction.

There are colleges in the United States offering courses on witchcraft, sorcery, and demonology; and these courses have an overflow attendance. How strange that it is not permitted to pray, worship God, or discuss the truth of the Bible in public educational institutions, but it is permitted to be involved with the powers of evil and to learn techniques for corrupting one's soul.

The full extent of satanic involvement will never be known. Much of it is done in secret vileness, in association with drugs and sexual abandonment. Occasional glimpses come to light in such horrors as the Manson murders and the ugly incident reported in the press in the summer of 1970. The latter was the murder of an innocent victim so that his heart could be cut out and eaten in some devilish orgy. No one who is alert to the world's present condition laughs today at the mythology of Satan. The whole idea may seem unreasonable and be unwanted; but the stark fact is that Satan is alive, he is out in the open, he is here to stay, and his powers increase daily.

The Bible is the only reliable source book for information concerning this being. Its words have existed for years, but the world has seen no relevance in its warnings. It is good now, in this time of satanic reality, to turn to the Word of God.

Ezekiel 28 is a chapter containing valuable information which is now confirmed in our drug culture. The prophet begins by describing an actual person living at that time, the prince of Tyrus. But soon his inspired words take on a special meaning and application.

The prince of Tyrus is being condemned because: "Thou hast said, I am a God. I sit in the seat of God" (v. 2). Ezekiel reveals an uncanny truth about this person: "Behold, thou art wiser than Daniel; there is no secret that they can hide from thee" (v. 3).

Did you know that Satan knows all your secrets, that you cannot hide anything from him? This is why he can tempt you so successfully. He knows your weak spots; he knows the sin that does so easily beset you. He isn't all powerful and all knowing, but he knows enough of you and me to be able to bring us into sin and failure if we face him in our own strength.

In verse 13 the allusion to Satan becomes obvious: "Thou hast been in Eden the garden of God." This is in full accord with the teaching in Genesis 3.

One reason for the previous unbelief in the reality of Satan was the caricatures of his physical appearance. The Middle Ages presented Satan as the epitome of ugliness; he was black, horned, with hoofs for feet, and a forked tail. He was understood to be repulsive because of this awful ugliness. People were afraid of him for his terrifying appearance. No wonder the educated person scoffed. But this medieval monstrosity isn't what the Bible teaches. The picture of Satan given in Ezekiel 28 is the very opposite, one of outstanding, unearthly beauty.

Reading further, we find in verse 13 a description of the appearance of Satan. Unusual words are used to describe the colors of this being. The Bible does not refer to colors such as purple or red or green; these are not vivid enough. It lists a series of precious stones as the covering of Satan: the sardius or ruby, topaz, the diamond, the beryl or chrysolite, the onyx, jasper, the sapphire, the emerald or chrysoprase, the carbuncle and gold. The quality of vivid flashing lights, many colored and ever changing with each movement, made the appearance of Satan. How different from the black ugliness of man's caricature. In keeping with the thought of unusual beauty, verse 17 tells us, "Thine heart was lifted up because of thy beauty." This unusual beauty was one of the causes of his destruction.

It is worth pausing here and underlining the truth of these last words. There are many girls who wish they were beautiful, and many young men, and older men too, who wish they were handsome. Each one dreams of how more exciting life would be if only they had that extra quality of physical beauty. To all such, the Bible gives a special word. Beauty can be a curse. It can lead to untold pressures and promote false values. The most beautiful created being was led on into destruction by his beauty. It might be wise to stop and thank God that you are not radiantly beautiful or magnificently handsome. Many who possessed these attributes have found life to be nothing but a snare and a delusion.

We have said that the rise of the modern drug culture is linked with the new emergence of Satan. We will see this in various ways in this first chapter. Notice, for example, the flashing colors of Satan's appearance, as noted in verse 13.

Now consider one of the popular occupations in the drug culture: blaring hard-rock bands playing in a room where psychedelic colors are made to whirl and flash. The whole experience bombards the ears with sounds too loud and blinds the eyes with lights too vivid, overwhelming the senses.

In such circumstances the individual exposed to this two-fold attack is literally forced to give in to a stronger power. Powers of resistance and rational understanding are steadily crushed under the force. The mind is left cracked and open to the invasion of superstimulating suggestions. Moral values disappear, and the listener is swallowed up in a new world of passion and sensation. This sensual bombardment, plus the use of drugs, however simple, leads to a disintegration of the character. All this is part of the plan of Satan in this present age.

We know that Jesus is the Light of the world. This is what He said in John 8:12. Now we have this distraction—Satan is the psychedelic, blinding light of the world. The contrast is between purity and perdition.

Further information concerning the person of Satan is found in verses 14 and 15 of this chapter of Ezekiel. The whole emphasis here is that he was a created being, perfect in his ways from the day that he was created until iniquity was found in him.

He held high office in the economy of God. He was higher than the angels, greater than the archangels. There is an amazing verse in Jude, verse 9, which tells of a contention between Michael the archangel and Satan. They were disputing about the body of Moses, but even Michael dared not deal with the enemy. Even he had to commit the issue to the Lord, whose power alone is sufficient to deal with the matter.

Ezekiel thus informs us about the person and power of the one who initiated rebellion. If we turn to Isaiah 14, we can find further details of the act which precipitated the whole tragedy of world rebellion.

Isaiah 14:12 begins: "How art thou fallen from heaven, O Lucifer, son of the morning!" Here again the name Lucifer tells of his brightness. This name means the bright shining one. Here is a comment on a recorded fact in heaven's history, the fall of Satan. When we take the information and put it alongside the words of our Lord in Luke 10:18, we have a phenomenal statement. From out of the depths of His heavenly experience, Jesus, speaking to the returning seventy disciples, said, "I beheld Satan as lightning fall from heaven." This is a glimpse into the hidden history of heaven. Jesus was there when it happened—think of that! He saw the arrogant rebel flung out of the place of grace and obedience. His eyes took in the whole scene. Consider the purpose of the Holy Spirit in recording these words for us, just a simple remark of Jesus in reply to the seventy. They had just returned from their mission with joy, and their comment had been one of amazement: "Even the devils are subject unto us through thy name." They spoke of the lesser demons, and Jesus spoke of the leader, the prince of hell.

Isaiah 14:13-14 then reveals the sin for which Satan was rejected from heaven: "For thou hast said in thine heart." We do not know when this took place; it is not recorded in human history. We simply know the facts as they are given to us. Somehow there was a working in the heart of this beautiful, created being. He had great power and authority, but this did not satisfy him. "Much wanted more." Once again we want to ask questions: "Why did God allow it?" "Didn't God know?" "Why didn't God stop him?" But again we find no answers. Once more the Bible tells us what we *need* to know, not what we *want* to know!

It is worth comparing the words quoted above with the opening words of Psalm 14: "The fool hath said in his heart, there is no God." Again there is an attitude of heart leading to an act of rebellion. Notice that Satan's opening attitude of heart has echoed down the years of human experience.

Then follows in Isaiah the words spoken in the heart of Satan. If we examine these phrases, we find a series of five statements each beginning with the words "I will." Every word in his heart was in opposition to God. Previous to this outburst, he had been perfect in his ways. His life had been one of true obedience to God. His very will had been subject to the will of God. But now the rebellion broke forth. He wanted to ascend, to exalt his throne, to sit; and, finally, he spoke the ultimate blasphemy: "I will be like the most High."

The five "I wills" are the cry of the rebel seeking to move out of dependence on God to complete independence. This is where rebellion began, in heaven itself. The rebellion actually was a determination to step into independence, to be free from the authority of God and to move into opposition against God.

For this rebellion, Jesus saw Satan as lightning fall from heaven. There were lesser angelic beings who supported him and went with him. We read of these in Jude 6: "And the angels which kept not their first estate [or their proper place], but left their own habitation, he hath reserved in everlasting chains under darkness unto the judgment of the great day."

This then was the first day of independence, the day when an opposition arose which was to set itself in full battle array against God. This was the seed which grew and blossomed and reproduced itself a million, million times in the human hearts to come. This one seed was to lead to all the sins, the sufferings, the wars, the miseries, the tragedies, the loneliness, the heartaches that have stained and saturated the broken hearts of humanity down the ages.

2

THE INVASION OF PLANET
EARTH

IN THE FIRST CHAPTER we saw that the rebellion which fills the
world today did not actually originate in this world.

When we read Genesis 1, we see no sign or hint of rebellion. Instead, in the closing verse, we read this: "And God
saw everything that he had made, and, behold, it was very
good." There is no opposition present.

As we go on into Genesis 2, again there is nothing contrary
to the will of God. There is a lovely picture of fellowship
between God and His creatures. We read that God provided
the perfect setting for man, that God and man worked together in happy communion: the whole scene is a blessed
picture of peace. The One we see here is the God of love,
providing for His loved ones, fellowshiping with His loved
ones.

One point is worthy of mention here: what was the basis
of this fellowship? We know that God is love; this is ever so,
ever will be so. But there is only one thing that will truly
satisfy love. Ask any true sweetheart of any age. Only love
in return can satisfy a heart that loves.

We can command obedience and force our will on others,
but we can never demand love in return. If it came that way,
it would not be true love. Love must be freely given without
any sense of coercion.

In order to express love there must be a choice possible,

a choice to love or not to love. This choice allowed the blessed fellowship in the Garden.

Verses 16 and 17 tell of the tree of the knowledge of good and evil. This was a tree of choice—the first tree of choice. (A second tree of choice appears later on in history.)

God gave to His loved ones the fruits of every tree in the Garden. Of these there were many, and the selection was varied and satisfying. But God used the tree of the knowledge of good and evil for a special purpose as a unique challenge. God said they should not eat of this tree, the only tree on which He put an embargo. As they abstained from this tree's fruit, they would be demonstrating not only their obedience to God but their love to Him. So simple to understand, so easy to fulfill. Just as we read from the lips of Christ in John 14:15: "If ye love me, keep my commandments."

This obedience was the basis of the wonderful fellowship that existed in the Garden. Love was seen and known and enjoyed. How long this blessed fellowship existed we do not know. All we do know is that the heart of God found a unique joy with those whom He had created. And thus it was until the events recorded in Genesis 3.

These opening chapters of Genesis are precious words. In a sense we are treading on holy ground as we follow the footsteps of God in relation to His loved ones. But these opening chapters are also persecuted words. These chapters are mocked and derided. No supposedly educated person can believe the events really happened. These words are written off as folklore—pleasant stories, but utterly worthless in historical value. Even many Christians do not know where they stand in their acceptance of the early Genesis chapters.

The theory of evolution—it really is only a theory—has been accepted as fact. As a result, all that develops from the creation story is treated as mythical. There is a good reason for this accepted attitude of unbelief. We will understand it more as this chapter continues. The real person behind the attack on the truth of God's Word is not the atheistic scholar or scientist but Satan himself. Jesus called him the father of lies: "When he speaketh a lie, he speaketh of his own: for he is a liar, and the father of it" (John 8:44*b*). Satan has developed and encouraged this attitude toward the opening chapters of Genesis for a good reason. By preparing people's hearts before they approach the teaching, he is laying a smoke screen to cover his own tracks. Satan would love to get Genesis 3 removed from the Bible for one special reason. In this chapter we see the plan and purpose of Satan in his attack in the Garden and the unique pattern he follows in all his assaults on men.

When a person accepts the story as pure myth, then he doesn't trouble to profit from it in his daily living. Who would want to live his life instructed by a fairy story? And so, no one pauses in chapter 3 to apply it to living. Men begin their purposeful Bible study with Abram; at least there did exist a place called Ur of the Chaldees. They can feel their feet on solid ground with Abram and Ur; who wants the old legends?

Thus Satan fulfills his plan. If people must have a Bible, then let them have a carefully expurgated edition.

As we look now into the teaching of Genesis 3, we will experience insights opposite to what Satan would promote. This is not a legend handed down by generations of imaginative enthusiasts, but it is as up-to-date in its teaching and applicability as tomorrow is. The events described have their counterparts happening day by day in every country. The temptations and the choices we meet in our daily lives, we view for ourselves in this tragic story.

Understand that this is the story of the first invasion of planet earth by a hostile power. Satan was in open opposition to God, but he had no power or capacity to hurt God personally. What he did was to strike at God through the ones whom God loved and created. There was a sweet fellowship existing in the Garden. If Satan could only break the bonds of that fellowship and cause these two in the Garden to step out into independence, just as he had done on that fateful day in heaven, then God would lose something which was precious to Him. Satan cared nothing for the suffering that would follow; all he wished to accomplish was a breakdown in the holy communion between God and man.

Now we can see how the battle is set up and study the techniques of this master spirit. This is how he moves against us.

The first six verses teach three things concerning Satan—his tactics, his teaching, his temptation.

Notice the clever *tactics* of the enemy as he approached the woman. He came in beauty and wonderful attraction, qualities we saw about him in chapter 1. This was no being to be feared, but one whose very manner was full of earnest concern and solicitude.

He opened his conversation by referring to the God known to both of them: "Yea, hath God said, Ye shall not eat of every tree of the garden?" Notice the carefully planned attack on the word of God. He began by casting a doubt on God's word: "Hath God said." There was no open denial; that would come later on. First, doubt was quietly raised.

Because there was no resistance to the doubt, he quickly followed up with an outright denial: "Ye shall not surely die." These words were a deliberate attack on the person and authority of God. Here we have the strange situation of the father of lies denouncing the God of all truth and accusing Him of giving wrong information to the two He created. But the woman made no effort to give God His rightful place.

This simple incident teaches us much about the tactics of Satan. First, that he begins with casting doubts on the Word of God; then, if the doubts are not dealt with, he goes on to a deliberate denial of the Word of God. We can see the same approach in the story of the temptation of Jesus in the wilderness. Matthew tells it this way in chapter 4, verse 3: "And when the tempter came to him, he said, If thou be the Son of God." Here again is the initial approach, "*If* thou be." Our Lord went on to deal with this doubt by simply using the Word of God: "It is written." The Word of God is its own sure defence.

We can see Satan's original tactics brought to perfection in many churches and seminaries today. Satan has no need to go around personally bringing first a doubt and then a denial of the Bible, the Word of God. He has men and women who do his work for him everyday. There are many places where a man will stand up with a Bible in his hand, but not to read or expound it. He says words like these: "Does the Bible really mean this? Is this what it is teaching?" First he sows a field full of doubts, then he goes on to water the seed. He says, "No! The Bible doesn't mean this; it means this." In saying so he cancels out the true teaching and substitutes a denial of God's Word. He sows the seeds of doubt, waters and fertilizes them by denial, and then leaves his listeners to harvest a crop of empty words from which no bread of life can be made. Some teachers will have much to answer for when they stand before the Lord in the day of judgment.

Having used these tactics to exalt himself at the expense of the honor of God, Satan then goes on to spell out his own perfidious *teaching*. We love to refer to John 3:16 as the gospel in a nutshell. We can now turn our attention to Genesis 3:5, the devil's gospel, which he proclaimed in the Garden with such remarkable success. This is the same program he uses today, has used throughout the years, with the same continuing success. It is sad that, in the world as a whole, the devil is seeing greater response to his gospel than that seen by faithful preachers of God's truth.

Over the past ten years I have had much opportunity to work with young people on the West Coast of the United States, especially in the state of California. I have worked with them in church meetings, in youth conferences, in individual speaking and counselling sessions. I have come to understand something of the tensions and temptations that these young people face. I have spoken with many Christians of high school and college age, and they have shared with me the relentless and insidious attacks made on them to draw them away from their faith.

All that they have told me is simply an expanded version of Genesis 3:5. The same satanic thrust is there with the same careless concern for what happens to the victims of his lie. Let me show you the final result of Satan's attack in figures that speak for themselves. Here is a quotation from a filmstrip produced by a nonreligious group, Constructive Action, Inc. It is from a message called *Pot, Rock, and Revolution.* It is dealing, as the title implies, with the tremendous attack on youth through the medium of drugs. These figures are for five years ending in 1969: "In the United States alone, 100,000 young people (two and one-half times the United States' Vietnam war deaths) have been killed by drugs, and far more have been converted into mental cripples."

Since 1969 there has been a merciful decrease in the Vietnam deaths but an increase in death by drugs among young people. This is all joy for Satan—the heartache, the shame, the utter uselessness of it all. What a price for a nation to pay, all for the thrill of an act of rebellion in the name of freedom and independence!

As I share with you the devil's gospel, let me do so in terms of the experiences of these Christian young people, as it is presented to them.

Here is the gospel of Satan in verse 5: "For God doth know that in the day ye eat thereof, then your eyes shall be opened, and ye shall be as gods, knowing good and evil."

There are three exciting experiences offered here by Satan, but notice first the way he introduces his teaching. He says:

"For God doth know." See the satanic subtlety in these four words. "Here is something God knows, but you don't know. God is keeping something back from you. Why hasn't He told you? Here is something you ought to know." See how Satan uses the name and authority of God to back up the temptation he is now about to present. In a way it comes with all the authority of God, but it comes through the lips of Satan, and the main point in the introduction is, "You are missing something that could be yours!"

Then he produces his first *temptation*: "Your eye shall be opened." And the young people say to me, "This is what our friends say, 'You Christian kids, you go around with your eyes closed. You haven't seen anything yet. You're like day-old kittens. Come with us and we'll really open your eyes. We'll show you things you never thought existed. Come with us and get your eyes opened.' "

I have also spoken with young men this last summer who had been hooked on hard drugs. In wonderful ways they had met Christ as their Saviour and had been delivered from the bondage of drugs. Speaking to me they said, "The exciting thing about drugs is what you see when you are turned on. You move into a new world of sight and seeing. Psychedelic colors twist and weave, flow and undulate; and you can see sounds." Satan is truly consistent in his temptation; his first appeal is to get your eyes open. Remember always, his aim is to entice them to want to have this experience. All they have to do is to take the fruit of the tree.

The second temptation he offered was, "Ye shall be as gods." Remember that this was the very cause of Satan's downfall as recorded in Isaiah 14:14: "I will be like the most High." Here he was getting down to the real business of being independent. If only they would take the fruit, they suddenly would become free. As it was, they were tied to God, and in bondage to Him. Fellowship was just another word for bondage. If only they would step out, they would be free to live their own lives, free to be gods in their own right.

The effectiveness of this message can be verified from the experiences of thousands of young people. They say the one clear call is to throw off all authority. "Why should the police tell you what to do? You are big enough to decide for yourself!" "Why should the school or college tell you what to do? You are old enough to choose for yourself!" "Why should your father tell you what to do? I don't let my parents dictate to me. Why should they tell you what time you have to be in? I don't tell my father." "You Christian kids, you're spineless. You just do what you are told. Stand up for your rights. Be a man. Run your own life your own way."

These are the constant pressures on Christian young people. If only they understood who is behind it, that this call to rebellion is a deliberate move on the part of Satan to hurt God. Once he has destroyed their witness and their love for God, he is utterly indifferent to what happens to them. Satan dangled before the eyes of these two in the Garden the glamour of freedom, but he never told them the price they would pay—they and all who would follow down through the years of time. To youth the act of defiance can seem brave and up-to-date; but it can lead on to a shambles of shame and horror, until one more name is added to the number of those who died for no cause at all and a fine boy or girl ends up as a statistic on a drug report.

Satan kept the most alluring temptation to the very last: "You will know good and evil." There never was an age in all the world's history like the present time, when this offer is so manifestly proclaimed.

These young people report, "This is exactly what they say to us. They speak of the glory of evil. They say 'You Christian kids are just a bunch of goody-goodies. All you know is good. There's nothing exciting in being good. Why *good* is a dirty, four-letter word. Come with us and we'll show you evil. Man, evil is so exciting, so thrilling. There is the thrill of the unknown, of doing wrong, of avoiding being caught. It makes life worthwhile. Who wants to be stuck with being good when the whole world of evil is awaiting you?' "

How real and up-to-date is this gospel of Satan! Its appeal is so demanding. Everybody goes this way. Coupled with the temptation within is the brainwashing that continues day by day through every means of mass communication. Amazing to me is not how many youngsters fall into the pit of failure but that there are not many more. Thank God for His infinite grace and the quiet working of His Holy Spirit resisting the evil and strengthening the child of God.

The result of this attack by Satan is known to all. The two in the Garden responded to the challenge by taking the fruit of the tree of the knowledge of good and evil. In doing so they demonstrated their own will, they disobeyed the command of the Lord God, and they deliberately chose to step into independence. This act of rebellion began the activity of rebellion all around us today.

Taking the fruit was not the cause; the basis of rebellion was the deliberate willfulness that led to such a step. Satan had said in heaven, "I will be like the most High, I will be like God." He had said to the two in the Garden, "You will be like gods." This became their choice: "We will be like gods." Satan's initial act in heaven was reproduced in the lives of these two on earth. And so it has continued down the ages, even to such words as we read in Luke 19:14: "We will not have this man to reign over us."

Remember the real purpose of Satan in launching this attack was to hurt God, especially to destroy the sweet fellowship in the Garden. He achieved immediate success, for we read in verse 8 that the Lord God came to the Garden in the cool of the day, but those whom He loved were gone. Notice that God did not forsake man. God was where man left Him, alone in the Garden. This gives us a beautiful picture of the seeking God. This is how God began and is yet today, always seeking the lost. This is what Jesus said in Luke 19:10. "For the Son of man is come to seek and to save that which was lost." Thank God for His amazing love that seeks and continues to seek.

The bitter end of this tragedy is seen in the events following verse 8. The Lord God came, but no one was there. Then He called to Adam and said to him, "Where art thou?" Back came the reply of the rebel from his hiding place among the trees in the Garden. See the beginning of bitterness and sorrow in these first recorded words of man: "I heard thy voice in the garden, and I was afraid . . . and I hid myself" (Gen 3:10).

Here is the first mention of fear in the Bible. There was no fear in chapter 1; everything was very good. There was no fear in chapter 2; everything was fellowship. It is in chapter 3 following the act of rebellion, that there creeps into the human vocabulary the word for the emotion which has the whole world in bondage. Fear is uppermost in the world today. Whichever country I visit, fear is written across the economy of the country, the relationship of the people, and the daily experience of the individual.

The price of rebellion and independence is bitterness and humiliation.

The invasion of the planet Earth was a great success. The devil could truly write "mission accomplished" across his record book. Fellowship was destroyed, man was driven out into the agony of existence, God was lonely, and all hell rejoiced.

But where sin abounded, grace did much more abound. That is the next part of our story.

3

GOD'S ANSWER

THIS REBELLIOUS STEP into independence started sin in the human heart. Romans 14:23 gives us an inclusive definition of what sin really is: "For whatsoever is not of faith is sin." Faith is complete reliance upon God alone and obedience to His Word. Therefore, if an act is not of faith, if it is not done in dependence on God, it is sin. Any act or decision made by a deliberate choice of human will, apart from dependence upon God, is sin.

This is why worry, fear, anxiety, and frustration are sins in the fullest sense. They come to the soul that chooses to face the problems of life all alone. Certainly, the sufferer may *speak* of his trust in God, of how God is the only answer to his need; but words are not actions. James 1:22 has the answer: "But be ye doers of the word, and not hearers only, deceiving your own selves."

The great outcome from this first act of rebellion in the Garden was guilt. God was the One against whom the affront had been committed, but who was going to find the answer to the problem of sin? Shouldn't it be man, the guilty one, who should provide the remedy and work out that which would restore the situation? But man was bankrupt, morally and spiritually. His previous assets of joy and peace had been his by dependence upon God. But now he was away from God, a stranger in a strange land, facing new and frustrating situations. He possessed nothing with which to make his way back to God. Certainly the answer to the problem of sin would not be found in human ability.

26

The answer, we know, came from God, the One against whom the sin had been committed. The One who loved in the Garden still loved in the hour of failure. This is the great significance of John 3:16: "For God so loved the world, that he gave his only begotten Son, that whosoever believeth in him should not perish, but have everlasting life." This verse is bigger than many people imagine. It is dealing with God's answer to the whole outcome of sin. We need to understand that two issues must be faced when we consider the effect of sin. First, there is the penalty of sin; second, there is the power of sin. It is not enough to provide a means whereby sin can be forgiven. This is essential, and it is the first issue to be faced; but there must also be provided a way by which sin can be resisted. We need an answer to the penalty of sin; but, equally important, we need an answer to the power of sin.

This is exactly what John 3:16 is saying. God so loved that He gave His only begotten Son for a twofold purpose. First, that whosoever would believe should not perish. He would be delivered from the penalty of sin as told in Ezekiel 18:4, "the soul that sinneth, it shall die." One purpose in the mind of God for giving His Son was that man might not die eternally as a result of the penalty of sin.

The second purpose was that man might have life, might possess a new capacity to meet the power of sin, and have new resources to live the life God intended him to live.

If God had only provided the answer to the penalty of sin, then man would be saved; but his daily life would be an experience of failure. Remember, God never saved you to be a failure, never saved you to be washed up on the shores of heaven. He is the giver of every good and perfect gift. His salvation is good and perfect (complete). God saved you so that you could really live. The tragedy is that so many Christians do not live; they just exist, conscious of their own failure and total inability to match up to the pressures of life.

In this chapter we will consider in wider detail God's answer to the penalty of sin. In the next chapter we will see how God, in an amazing way, has provided the answer to the power of sin in our daily lives.

We saw in the first chapter of this book that the rebellion began in heaven. In just the same way the redemption also began in heaven. We can read this in 1 Peter 1:19, 20. Here we see that we were redeemed, "with the precious blood of Christ, as of a lamb without blemish and without spot: Who verily was foreordained before the foundation of the world, but was manifest in these last times for you."

In the inscrutable economy of the Trinity, worked out before this world was ever formed, there was the complete plan of redemption. Father, Son, and Holy Spirit designed and foreordained the glorious mystery of human redemption before there was a human or even a world. The whole concept baffles human intelligence. We can see now that when man fell and sin came in, God was not caught unprepared. There was no panic in heaven. Satan could write across his attack "Mission accomplished," but God was ready with the answer to it all—"Operation Redemption."

This divine plan included aspects which cause dissension among many so-called Christians today. For example, the whole basis for forgiveness is found in Hebrews 9:22: "Without shedding of blood is no remission [or forgiveness]."

Over recent years great resentment has arisen against this concept. It is cried down as being a religion of the slaughterhouse, revolting and unlovely. In some denominations all the hymns referring to the blood of Christ have been removed. This is sad and presumptuous on the part of sinful creatures, however important they may be. They say the idea of the shedding of blood is not nice. This is true. But then, sin itself is not nice; there is nothing lovely about the shame and ugliness of a life stained and broken by sin. The real point is that blood sacrifice is the way God chose to deal with sin.

If one of these dissenters had been God, maybe he would have found another way for dealing with sin—and even try to improve upon unpleasant events of life, such as birth and death. But such a man isn't God, he is just one of the many sinners who need to be saved.

This is what God chose, whether we like it or not! The amazing thing is that God not only chose the way, He provided the way, in Christ. In contemplating the last thought we begin to see the immeasurable grandeur of God's love. Not only did He undertake to find the way back for sinful man, but He Himself paid the price. Compare the glorious grandeur of John 3:16 with the dramatic words of 1 John 3:16, "Hereby perceive we the love of God, because he laid down his life for us." The wonder of it all—"that God was in Christ reconciling the world unto himself." (2 Co 5:19).

Always remember that when we are talking about the blood of Christ, we are not speaking of a theological issue but of a physical reality. His blood was shed, and His side was pierced. It was actual blood flowing from His veins, but it was the blood of God—amazing thought!

There are others who, when discussing the concept of "without shedding of blood is no remission," will say, "but this was only for the Old Testament." Such people need to be reminded that Hebrews 9:22 is in the New Testament and also that the verb is in the present tense: "*is* no remission of sins." We need to be fully aware of the fact that even today God only forgives sin on the basis of shed blood.

This is why the Bible, from cover to cover, accepts and knows no other way, even in the glory of heaven itself: "In the midst of the throne . . . in the midst of the elders, stood a Lamb as it had been slain" (Rev 5:6). And the continual song of those in verse 9 is "for thou wast slain, and hast redeemed us to God." Verse 12 adds the glorious words of worship: "Worthy is the Lamb that was slain to receive power, and riches, and wisdom, and strength, and honour, and glory, and blessing." If we count up in the book of Revelation we find the word *Lamb* with the capital L, coming twenty-eight times. Each reference is to Christ and His shed blood. In fact, the whole New Testament has only five more references to the word *lamb,* and four of them are used concerning the Lord Himself. How significant is the truth contained in that precious word.

If we turn to Leviticus 4, we have set out before us the method used in the Old Testament for the forgiveness of sins. This chapter tells the mechanics of forgiveness, the procedure to be followed by the sinner in his need. This method was the one and only way by which sins were forgiven. It was given early in the history of the Jewish relationship with God, and it continued in use down to the days of our Lord.

Leviticus 4 describes the plan to be followed by four different groups: "If the priest that is annointed do sin" (v. 3) ; "If the whole congregation . . . sin" (v. 13) ; "When a ruler hath sinned" (v. 22) ; and "If any one of the common people sin" (v. 21). Four groups are mentioned because different animals had to be brought according to each group, but the method of obtaining forgiveness was the same in each case.

If we consider the case of one of the common people, we can see the plan for all. In fact, we can see, in a sense, the method God uses for the forgiveness of sins, even today.

The Bible tells that such a man would have a sense of sin on his soul. He would feel the guilt and the increasing sense of separation from God. Then he would initiate steps to seek forgiveness and cleansing. He went to his flock and selected an animal without any blemish. In this way he deprived himself of his own possessions; it cost him something. He carried the little animal on his shoulders to the tabernacle, or, later on, to the temple. There he met a priest who would recognize the purpose of his visit.

The man would then begin the process leading up to forgiveness. He placed his hands on the head of the animal and confessed before God the burden and guilt of his soul. By doing this, he was transferring his own sin to the sinless sacrifice. When his confession was ended, he would take his knife and kill the animal there in the presence of the priest. The priest then took the blood of the dying animal and put it on the horns of the altar of burnt offering. When the priest had ended his part in the burning of the sacrifice, he turned to the man and told him two amazing things: first, that an atonement had been made for the man's sin, and that his sin had been forgiven.

On hearing these words, the man returned to his home with his heart rejoicing—his burden of sin was gone. If you had asked the man the secret of his newfound joy, he would have told you that his sin was forgiven. If you had asked him further if he understood how his sin was forgiven, he would have no explanation other than that this was the way Jehovah had decreed. Trusting and obedience had brought the forgiveness and cleansing.

In the process of time this same man would once again be conscious of sin and guilt. Once more he would go through the same ritual, and once more, the shed blood brought him two things—an atonement and forgiveness.

Thus it was in the life of one man, and this procedure was multiplied many thousands and millions of times in the lives of many Jews down through the years of time until the days of Christ.

In this process of forgiveness, one word deserves special notice, the word *atonement*. Its actual meaning is a covering. This chapter teaches that the blood of the animal covered the sin in the sight of God. The sin remained in all its ugliness, but it was covered by the blood. God saw it no more. As a result, the sin that he had committed was forgiven him.

In this way all the millions of sacrifices for sins would have played their part in the covering of all the sins. None of these many sins were gone—they all remained—but they were covered by the blood.

Thus it continued until the glorious day mentioned in John 1:29: "The next day John seeth Jesus coming unto him, and saith, Behold the Lamb of God, which taketh away the sin of the world." What a tremendous day this was. Here was coming the fulfillment of that unique plan designed in heaven before the world began.

Notice what Jesus was going to do. By His shed blood He was going to *take away* the sin of the world. That is why on the cross, just before He dismissed His spirit, He cried, "It is finished." John 19:30 says: "He said, It is finished: and he bowed his head, and gave up the ghost." "Bowed his head" is a special phrase, signifying a deliberate putting of the head into a position of rest. He had successfully accomplished that for which He was on the cross; He had taken away the sin of the world.

Now see the glory and the grandeur of the cross of Christ. There are some who say, "I don't see how Jesus dying nearly two thousand years ago could forgive my sins." It is much more wonderful than that. The cross of Christ stands at the center of all time here on this earth. Every sacrifice offered under the plan of Leviticus 4 looked forward to the cross. Every animal that died was a picture and type of Christ—up to a point. Its blood was shed, but the shed blood did not remove the sin from the sight of God. The sin remained, covered, waiting for Him who was the Lamb of God. No wonder every saint who ever lived can say, "In the cross of Christ I glory."

See now the sad affront offered to God by such as deny and despise the blood of Christ. They are out of tune with heaven and out of touch with God. They have nothing left as an offering for sin except the so-called goodness of their miserable, sin-stained lives. What a pitiful contrast this makes against the magnificent glory of the cross and its blood.

Hebrews 10 has much to say about the success and failure of the offerings made in the tabernacle. Verse 4 teaches, "For it is not possible that the blood of bulls and of goats should take away sins." Here again it establishes the truth of the atonement or covering value of the Jewish sacrifices. They could not take away sin, only cover them. Verse 10 gives us the truth of the "once for all" offering of Christ: "We are sanctified through the offering of the body of Jesus Christ once for all." Verse 12 speaks of "one sacrifice for sins for ever."

Remember, in this chapter we have been considering God's answer to the penalty of sin. Man through his rebellion became a sinner; and through his continued life of independence, he remains a sinner in the sight of God. Because he is a sinner, he needs an answer to the penalty of his sin. He needs to be saved so that he will not suffer eternal death.

We have just considered God's answer as depicted in the Old Testament plan. We need now to be reminded again that "without shedding of blood is no remission." We need to see how this great truth can be realized and enjoyed.

Someone may say, "What do I do today? I have no lamb to bring; and even if I had a lamb, where would I take it?" There is no need to seek for a lamb; God has provided the one Lamb of God. There is no need to seek for a temple because there is no need for any further offerings. Jesus was the one sacrifice for sins forever. But there is a need for identification with the Lamb of God.

Under the law, the sinner brought his lamb, placed his hands upon its head, and identified himself and his sin with the lamb. We need to become involved with Christ in a personal and practical way. We must go individually to the cross and realize that Jesus was dying for each one of us personally. As Paul could say, "The Son of God, who loved me, and gave himself for me" (Gal 2:20).

We need to humble our hearts, confess and repent of our sin, and accept the Lamb of God as our one sacrifice for sins. When we so identify ourselves with the Lamb of God, accepting Him as our Saviour, pleading only the merits of His precious shed blood, then we too can enter into the joy of sins forgiven. Not because we understand it, but because in simple faith we are obedient to God's will. Our enjoyment is greater than that in the Old Testament. Their sin was only covered, but our sin is gone for ever, taken away by the blessed Lamb of God.

Most of you reading this book will have made this decision, maybe years ago. But there may be just one who has never really come to the cross and made a personal identification with the Lamb of God. May I suggest that you consider carefully your present condition. God has planned your salvation. Christ has died to make it effective. Would you come as in Leviticus 4 and place your hands, by faith, on the Lamb of God? If you do this in all sincerity, then you, too, can know forgiveness and cleansing—and the joy of the Lord will fill your heart.

4

GOD'S WILL

So FAR WE HAVE SEEN what rebellion is, where it began, who started it all, and how it invaded this world. We have learned that rebellion is sin because it is the act of being independent of God. This independence is seen not only in the nonbelieving world, but in the heart of every Christian. It is the natural state of the human heart. It is also the constant attitude of what the Bible calls "the flesh." Here we need to be reminded what "the flesh" really is. We know it includes all the wicked and sinful practices of the heart, but it is more. A good definition of "the flesh" is this: "All that a person is without Christ." We need to remember that the flesh can also be gracious and charming. Some non-Christians have a sweetness and loveliness of character that outshine that of many Christians. This is part of their psychological makeup, just as some people are naturally physically beautiful; it is no special indication of the indwelling Spirit.

The end product is always the same: the flesh, attractive or unattractive, is in rebellion against God. Romans 8:7-8 puts it this way: "The carnal mind [the flesh] is enmity against God: for it is not subject to the law of God, neither indeed can be. So then they that are in the flesh cannot please God."

It is in this area of the flesh that the power of sin finds its full activity.

In our last chapter we saw how God, and God alone, found the answer to the penalty of sin. He gave His Son to be the Lamb of God. In this chapter we are specially concerned with the other terrible product arising from the initial act of rebellion, the power of sin. This is where there is great ignorance in Christian experience, yet there is need for victory over the power of sin.

Every true Christian is saved. He knows his sins are forgiven. He rejoices in the finished work of Christ. He realizes he is born again. In other words, he is fully conscious of God's answer to the penalty of sin. A great tragedy in the church is that this is *all* many Christians know. Thank God for every precious soul who has come to the cross and found redemption in Christ; but, oh that all believers might know God's answer to the power of sin day by day.

Practically all my counselling sessions are with Christians who are truly saved but whose lives are bound up in failure, fear, frustration, and a total inability to live the Christian life. They have had a true experience of the initial step of salvation, but they know nothing of the day by day activity of salvation. This is the number one problem in the church today. If this could be corrected right in the place where all the problems start, the human heart, then most of the other issues and problems arising would all be taken care of.

In considering the wonderful way by which God has provided the answer to the power of sin in human experience, we must direct our attention to the first chapter of Ephesians. This epistle is full of teaching concerning conduct and behavior in the church. It has much to say in the context of the home and the relationships therein. But before it ever directs the believer's mind to his personal walk, it focuses his attention on the will of God for daily witness. It is this will of God that needs to be understood and obeyed.

Every believer, if questioned, would admit his desire to do the will of God. No one would ever deny the importance of the will of God. So let us test our sincerity by seeing what that will is, and how far we have responded to it.

If you were to read the first fourteen verses of chapter 1,

you would find three references to the will of God: verse 5 speaks of "the good pleasure of his will"; verse 9 says "Having made known unto us the mystery of his will"; verse 11 tells of "him who worketh all things after the counsel of his own will."

Understanding these three references will go a long way toward solving the failure in many Christian lives. To get a better grasp of the layout of the will of God, I suggest you make these three verses into a simple diagram. Make a heading at the top of your diagram and put there these words: "the counsel of his own will." Then, below this one heading place the two subheadings, side by side: "the good pleasure of his will" and "the mystery of his will."

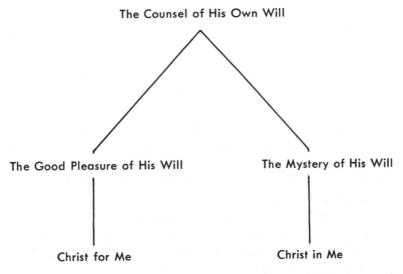

We can see first that "the counsel of God's will" for each believer is a twofold thrust in the life. These two together, "the good pleasure of his will" and "the mystery of his will," make up the actual total counsel of God's will. If only one part of the will has been obeyed, then one part has been left unfulfilled. This actually happens in many lives—a partial fulfillment of the will of God. This involvement with only half the will of God is what leads to so much failure in meeting the power of sin.

We will see this now as we continue with our diagram. Let us take each section separately. See what is "the good pleasure of his will" in verses 6 and 7: "In whom we have redemption through his blood, the forgiveness of sins, according to the riches of his grace."

The purpose of our study in chapter 3 was to see how God met the penalty of sin by sending the Lamb of God. We have no need to deal with that subject again, except to note in passing that the purpose of "the good pleasure of God's will" was to save us from the penalty of sin. Every true believer understands the necessity for the cross. We have all accepted Christ as our Savior, therefore being obedient to "the good pleasure of his will."

But, how about being involved with "the mystery of his will"—have you given equal obedience in this area of Christian living? There are many Christians who would be unable to give a sure answer to this challenge. Unable, not because they have chosen to disregard the will of God, but because, in many cases, they are completely ignorant as to what is the mystery of God's will.

Some folk when pressed to give an answer would say, "Well, it's a mystery, so how can you be expected to understand it!" They see the word "mystery" and almost automatically pass over the statement. They find the ordinary Word of God a big enough problem without going into such areas which are specifically called mysteries.

But notice what happens if this is your attitude. First, you have only been obedient to half of the will of God. Second, besides this disobedience, you leave untouched and unexplored the vast new area of tremendous potential for Christian living. It is this last deficiency that is at the root of so much ineffective and flabby Christian witnessing.

Let us search deeper into God's Word and find more information about this great area of the will of God.

There are two other places in the New Testament where we can discover additional information concerning the mystery of God's will. Turn your attention first to Romans 16: 25-26. Paul, under the leading of the Holy Spirit, has finished his letter and added the benediction. Then he proceeds to write these words of penetrating truth: "Now to him that is of power to stablish you according to my gospel, and the preaching of Jesus Christ, according to the revelation of the mystery, which was kept secret since the world began, but now is made manifest, and by the scriptures of the prophets, according to the commandment of the everlasting God, made known to all nations for the obedience of faith."

There are three points here of importance. Notice first the information about the mystery itself. It *was* kept secret since the world began, but *now* it is made manifest. It is a secret no longer, nor a mystery. The curtain has been pulled aside and the mystery has been revealed. See what this means to every believer. We can no longer dismiss "the mystery of God's will" by saying we cannot be expected to understand it. We may use such words and follow this line of action, but we do so in contradiction to the revelation of God. If we want to insist on a noninvolvement in this area, then we have to find some other reason or promote some other excuse.

The second point to realize is the purpose of the revelation of this mystery. We can see this in the beginning of verse 25: "Now to him that is of power to stablish you . . . according to the revelation of the mystery." This mystery is linked with the preaching of the gospel. It is a vital part of the gospel because through this wonderful mystery the believer can be established, the greatest need in the church today. To be established means to have roots that go down deep so that in the time of testing the believer can stand.

I am writing these words in the Philippines, in the city of

Manila. Two months ago this city was hit by a typhoon, the severest in living memory. Winds up to 150 m.p.h. swept through this area and the damage resulting would have to be seen to be believed. There was much structural damage to buildings and light and power poles. But I was interested to see the casualties in the tree population. Rows of great trees were pushed over, and many more were broken and deformed. The interesting thing was to see trees standing where others around them had fallen. There are many reasons for such selective destruction, but practically all the trees that were down had root systems close to the surface. The roots had not gone down deep but had found their sustenance near the surface.

I find this is true of many Christians. They believe in having roots; they know that a Christian is like a plant and cannot grow without roots. But so many are like the trees that fell in Manila; their roots are near the surface. They, too, are content to draw on surface experiences for their spiritual growth. The roots that hold are the roots that go deep and entwine themselves in the rock and solid area far below the surface of life. It is quieter there also, and the temperature remains even with no damage from extreme heat or bitter frost and cold. There is also a better chance of finding water deep down, and water means life.

Verse 25 of Romans 16 tells us that the understanding of the mystery of God's will is one of the means of establishing the Christian. It will enable him to have roots that go deep and will hold him up in the times of testing.

The end of verse 26 gives us the third point in this passage dealing with the mystery of God's will. It was kept secret, but now it is made known to all nations, "for the obedience of faith." There is the challenge; it is made known so that we may be obedient to what God wills.

All believers have responded to "the good pleasure of God's will." Most gladly have we obeyed the call to come to the cross and receive forgiveness of sins; but how about the equally important mystery of God's will? Have we been obedient in that area, or have we dismissed the whole thought and given it no further consideration? If the latter has been our response, then we have been going against the known and revealed will of God.

It is this ignorance, or indifference, that is the root cause of so much feeble Christian living. Wherever I go, I see churches with members who are truly "born again," but their capacity to experience the living, vital faith is nil. No amount of programs or techniques or gimmicks will ever make a Christian stable and strong in times of stress within or without. Hanging decorations on a tree, tying fruit to its branches, or nailing notices to its trunk are no substitutes for roots. Only the tree can grow the roots and they must go downwards, unseen, unknown, not admired or praised, but there to provide comfort in the time of storm.

There is a second scripture passage speaking about the mystery. I am looking in Colossians, chapter one, and reading verses 25 through 29.

As we begin to read these verses, we get a sense of something very special coming up. Paul, led by the Holy Spirit, writes words that seem to be boasting. He says he is made a minister of God "to fulfil the word of God," to complete the Word of God and make it fully known. Something has not yet been told, and God has anointed him to tell this special truth which will then complete the Word of God.

So we read on to find what this great truth really is: "Even the mystery which hath been hid from ages and generations, but now is made manifest to his saints." Here we are meeting the same teaching we saw in Romans 16:25-26. It is a mystery no longer, it is now revealed to all believers. At this point we should be careful to remember the words of our Lord in Mathew 18:16: "In the mouth of two or three witnesses every word may be established." Here are the two witnesses, written under the leading of the Holy Spirit, each saying the same thing—it is a mystery no longer.

Finally, we come to the telling forth of the mystery. Before spelling it out word by word, Paul uses extravagant words to try to capture the pinnacle position of this great truth: "the riches of the glory of this mystery." The mystery itself is supreme, as if it were a priceless piece of intricate jewelry. But then he points to the precious stone that lies at the center of the golden frame and there it is—God's greatest masterpiece —"Christ in you, the hope of glory."

This then, in simplicity, is the mystery of the will of God— "Christ in you." When we take this truth and place it in the simple diagrams we were using earlier in this chapter, we can see the buildup of blessing. First we had the overall heading, "the counsel of his own will," then the two sub-headings. The first one was "the good pleasure of his will," which was Jesus dying for me on the cross, in other words, "Christ for me." The mystery we have just seen is "Christ in me." Thus the twofold will of God becomes a realization first of "Christ for me," then of "Christ in me."

Remember why this will of God was so ordained. God was finding and supplying the answer to man's rebellion and sin. We saw that sin had a double result, the penalty of sin and then the power of sin. We can begin to understand now that the twofold will of God takes care of the twofold result of sin. Where sin abounded, grace did much more abound.

To the penalty of sin, which is the death of man the sinner, comes the answer: the death of Christ the Saviour, Christ for me!

To the power of sin, which is the constant downward pull exerted through a fallen human nature, comes the experience of participating in the divine nature with its constantly available power and victory, Christ in me!

Notice now another thought. Colossians 1:27 gave the mystery as, "Christ in you, the hope of glory." Realize that this is intended to be a present tense experience. This glory is not something we get only when we die and go to heaven, but is a hope of glory here and now. There will undoubtedly be great glory when we get to heaven, but we also have a promise of glory in this present rebellious world. See how this can become true in your own experience. Every true Christian believes in heaven as a place, but the exact geographical location is hard to determine—is it up, or down, or where? Perplexity is aggravated when you stand in New Zealand or Australia—is it still up, or down, or where?

We can be sure that where Jesus is, is heaven. He is the center of all the praise and glory of heaven. Now, if Christ really and truly indwells me, and heaven is where Jesus is, then, in some new and wonderful way, I can enjoy heaven on the way to heaven. This indwelling glory is the joyous birthright of every born-again believer. Regardless of circumstances or pressures or fears or any thing that this world may bring, we may know and experience a sweet, blessed, peaceful glory, day by day, as we recognize the Christ who indwells each of us in the person of His Holy Spirit.

There is another rich thought that follows directly. Only in this world do we have this experience of "Christ in me." When we get to heaven, we shall see Him as He is, and we shall be like Him—but He will not be the indwelling Christ. Only now is this our special blessing. Consider, how long have you left in your life: days, weeks, months, or years? For that time only has God given you this unique experience.

God has invested a rich deposit of blessing in the bank of your daily life. It is to last only while you are on earth. You can never overdraw your account because the power of Christ is limitless, but you can live your life without making a single withdrawal from the bank of blessing, and this is what many Christians do. They struggle to live for Jesus and make their own deposits in the bank of blessing, when all the time the will of God is that Christ should live in them and for them and through them. It is not a deposit account but a withdrawal account. It sounds totally impossible, but this is the will of God.

It is good at this time to compare this will of God, as detailed in our present chapter, with the will of Satan as we saw it in Isaiah 14 and in Genesis 3. Do you remember the five times that Satan said, "I will," culminating in the final blasphemous cry "I will be like God"? Then do you remember the second part of his gospel in Genesis 3:5, "You will be like gods"? Both statements show clearly the will of Satan, "I will be like God." Now consider the first part of the counsel of God's will, the good pleasure of His will. This divine desire we read of in Philippians 2:6-7: "Who, being in the form of God, thought it not robbery to be equal with God: but made himself of no reputation, and took upon him the form of a servant, and was made in the likeness of man." There it is, can you see it? God said, "I will be like man." What a fantastic contrast to the will of Satan!

But that isn't all. The second part of the counsel of God's will was the mystery of His will, and this, as we have seen, was that Christ should be in us, that we should be partakers of the divine nature. In other words, God said, "Man will be like me." What a deeply moving thought—"I will be like man," then "Man will be like me."

> O the depth of the riches both of the wisdom and knowledge of how unsearchable are his judgments, and his ways past finding out!
> For who hath known the mind of the Lord? or who hath been his counsellor?
> Or who hath first given to him, and it shall be recompensed unto him again?
> For of him, and through him, and to him, are all things: to whom be glory for ever. Amen (Ro 11:33-36).

How much do you know in your personal life of this will of God? Certainly you know salvation by the death of Christ;

this is the starting place for every true believer. But have you gone any further? Do you know the reality of Christ in you?

I find with many earnest Christians an honest realization of their present failure, a growing interest in the unfolding possibilities of a Christ-filled life, but an absolute barrenness when it comes to putting the truth to work. "If only I knew how to live this kind of life" is their cry.

This is the purpose of our next chapter—to study the mechanics of living the Christ-filled life.

5

GOD'S PLAN

THIS CHAPTER contains probably one of the most needed teachings for the church today. I say this not because I am writing it, but because of the truth in it I want to share.

There is much preaching which exhorts the believer to recognize the indwelling Christ, which tells him that Christ alone can give him victory. Such preaching then earnestly challenges the hearer to get into a deeper involvement with Christ so that the peace of God may fill his heart. All this is wonderful, true, and vitally necessary; but sadly, this is often where the message ends.

The hearer has been taught, challenged, and brought to a crisis moment of deep decision, but then what does he do? How does he do it? I remember once when I had been speaking to a group of college students. Their hearts were all fired up, and they were ready to go. Then as I concluded, one of them said, "Great, this is fine, just what we need, but how do we make it work? What are the mechanics of living a victorious life? Spell it out inch by inch!"

The greatest longing of many Christians is to have a victorious life. The believer may desire to make Christ real, but how to do so is the baffling problem. I want to share with you now God's plan for making God's total will a living reality in the experience of the believer.

I want to turn your attention to Romans 6:1-14. This section of Scripture tells quite clearly what is the plan in the mind of God whereby the mystery of God's will can become a motivating power.

46

It is interesting to compare how different people react to the truth of the indwelling Christ. Every born-again child of God has a belief in the indwelling Christ. It is part of our spiritual vocabulary in prayer and praise and song. We love to sing such words as, "You ask me how I know He lives, He lives within my heart!" It all sounds fine, very uplifting, and theologically correct, but what does it mean?

Sometimes I trace the thought patterns of teenagers. There are some who reason this way: "Jesus lives in my heart, He will take care of me whatever happens, so I will live my life as I see it, and as I want it, and I'll trust Jesus to take care of me." Their favorite hymn becomes, "He will take care of you," sung with a warm, comfortable feeling that whatever happens, whatever I do, somehow Jesus will keep me.

It isn't only teenagers who think like that, many adult Christians also have a nebulous concept of what Christian living means. There are many who just push on, do what they want, and expect Jesus to straighten things out for them.

I need to realize that before I became a Christian, there was just "me"—my fallen human nature, the flesh. After I became a Christian, I became a partaker of the divine nature; Jesus came to indwell me in the person and presence of His Holy Spirit. The flesh, remember, is "all that a person is without Christ," whether lovely or unlovely, gracious or ungracious. And it is in this area of the flesh that the power of sin is demonstrated and experienced.

As a Christian I now have two natures within me—a fallen human nature which is me, and the divine nature which is Christ. The whole problem of Christian living now turns on the relationship between these two natures. Who does what or who helps whom? Do I struggle on and do my best, then call in Christ to help me when I am in trouble? Or does Jesus take control and I help Him? Is it a demonstration of teamwork?

In understanding this relationship most Christians need

help. Romans 6 tells us what God's plan is for solving this
personal problem. Remember it was "God's answer" that
provided the Lamb of God to deal with the penalty of our
sin. It was "God's counsel" that devised the mystery of God's
will, whereby Christ would dwell in us to give us victory over
the power of sin. Now it is "God's plan" that enables us to
enjoy the success that God's will provided. Let us now see
what this plan is.

Verse 1 of Romans 6 poses a question: "What shall we say
then? Shall we continue in sin, that grace may abound?" Shall
I just go on living the same defeated life and let God's grace
take care of it all? Quite rightly so the next two words are
"God forbid." Then the chapter begins to teach three important facts.

There used to be a time when basic teaching given in
school was called the three R's—reading, 'riting, and 'rith-
metic. The Bible gives the three R's of basic Christian living;
we will discuss them one at a time. The first R is *realize*. The
first eight verses say that in God's sight, when Christ died on
the cross, I died. This comes as a shock, but here it is in the
Word. Verse 3 says, "Know ye not, that so many of us as were
baptized into Jesus Christ were baptized unto his death."
Verse 4 says, "We are buried with him by baptism into death
. . . even so we also should walk in newness of life." Verse 5
adds, "For if we have been planted together in the likeness of
his death, we shall be also in the likeness of his resurrection."
Verse 6 is very definite: "Our old man [fallen human nature]
is crucified with him." Verse 8 says, "Now if we be dead with
Christ, we believe that we shall also live with him." Notice
the emphasis: "with him" in verse 4, "together" verse 5, "with
him" in both verses 6 and 8.

God has finished with the flesh, as Romans 8:8 says: "So
then they that are in the flesh cannot please God." There is
nothing in human nature by itself which can satisfy the heart
of God. We are rebels, enemies of God; the heart is always a

rebel, and God has no plans for improving human nature. "Therefore if any man be in Christ, he is a new creature: old things are passed away; behold, all things are become new, and all things are of God" (2 Co 5:17, 18). We are new creatures because we have a new nature—the divine nature, Christ indwelling us.

If we accept this part of God's plan, then we can see straight away that some of our nebulous ideas must go. It won't be a case of my doing all I can for Christ, then calling Him in to help me over the hard spots. We will have to see ourselves in the context of Galatians 2:20, where Paul gives his own testimony to the truth we are at present considering. He says, "I am crucified with Christ: nevertheless I live; yet not I, but Christ liveth in me." Notice that Paul uses the same two words "with Christ," such as we have in this section. He accepts the great fact that when Christ died, he died. If he is crucified, the "he" being his fallen human nature, then he is out of the way. This is exactly what we are considering under the first R—Realize that when Christ died, I died.

A further glance at the verses we have quoted from Romans 6 reveal one other important fact. As well as saying that we are to realize that we have died with Christ, they also go on to underline the fact that "we should walk in newness of life," "should be in the likeness of His resurrection," "should also live with Him." This is a present-tense walk and a today experience. This is not something that will happen when I get to heaven; this is the "now" of my salvation. This is the demonstration of the "new creature," but it cannot take place until I first realize that "I" am out of the way. This is why so many of us never live like new creatures; we are always being fouled up by the old nature, either trying to help or hindering.

Now let us look at the second R, which is the word *Reckon.* We saw above that the teaching of the first eight verses is that in God's sight, when Christ died, I died. Notice those words:

in God's sight. This is essential truth in His planning. God has finished with human nature and sees only Christ.

Here the problem really hits us. It is one thing to say "in God's sight." He may have finished with human nature, but I have not finished with my human nature. I am stuck with it, and it will be with me as long as I live on this earth. All its failings and fears, all its temptations and potential for sin, all its rebellion and independence—these are mine. In this human nature the power of sin is experienced; this is my daily battleground. Even though God has finished with it, I have not.

This is where the mystery of God's will begins to reveal itself in all its amazing wisdom and matchless skill. God's Word in verses 10 and 11 says, "For in that he died, he died unto sin once: but in that he liveth, he liveth unto God. Likewise reckon ye also yourselves to be dead indeed unto sin, but alive unto God through Jesus Christ our Lord."

How do I handle a human nature which is in rebellion, which God has finished with? I proceed to finish with it my-self—not a once-for-all finishing, but a moment-by-moment, leading to a day-by-day experience. How do I finish with it? The word in verse 11 is "reckon ye also yourselves to be dead indeed unto sin." Reckon means "consider yourselves also dead to sin and your relation to it broken" (Amplified N.T.).

In other words, I should act as if I am dead to sin, I should behave as if I am insensible to its power.

This is not teaching sinless perfection, or putting forth the idea that I cannot sin. But it is saying, "I don't *have* to sin, I don't *have* to lose my temper, say those words, think those thoughts, do that act. I may sin and probably will, but I do not *have* to sin—there is a way out." This is the motivating thought, the hinge upon which the door of blessing will swing open to the touch.

Now, what do I do next when I count myself out of the situation? The truth comes in verse 13: "Neither yield ye your members as instruments of unrighteousness unto sin: but yield yourselves unto God, as those that are alive from the dead, and your members as instruments of righteousness unto God." The key word here is "yield." I have called it the third R—*Respond.* I yield, respond, become vitally involved with the other nature that indwells me, the divine nature. I switch off the old nature, consider it dead, and relate the issues of living to the new nature. In other words, I recognize the indwelling Christ as a real person, and I bring my bodily members and faculties to place at His disposal.

Let me explain this in another way, by bringing to your mind and your imagination visual concepts and practical considerations. I want to talk about making a new behavior pattern. We all have our own behavior pattern. It has grown and developed with us as our life continued. This is the old behavior pattern, the pattern that comes from our own human nature. We know how it will react in many cases, because that is exactly what it has been doing over the years of our life. Certain events will make us fearful, and other things will make us angry. To some items we respond with joyous delight, to others with utter bewilderment. Certain temptations will almost invariably cause us to give way to our natural impulses and we fall into sin. There is always "the sin which doth so easily beset us" (Heb 12:1).

Before we became Christians this old behavior pattern was the story of our life. There are those of us whose life was like a constant rerun of an old movie, like the constant repetition of a record played on the turntable of our heart. Most of us never realize the pattern we live, we just tread it out in the jangle of daily living.

But when we became Christians, we suddenly realized that we should begin to live a different kind of life. So, with all our sincerity and enthusiasm we started to live for Jesus. We proceeded to clean up our lives, to get rid of our bad habits, to remodel our whole method of living. What we were trying to do was to improve our old behavior pattern, to start and live the Christian life.

This is exactly what many Christians are busily engaged in at this moment. This is what they call living the Christian life. The tragedy is that it becomes increasingly difficult to improve the old behavior pattern. Our failure to do so only increases our guilt which then drives us to higher heights of endeavor to improve our old behavior pattern and make it acceptable to God.

Depending upon our age, sincerity, and enthusiasm, we keep on working at this impossible task until finally we accept defeat as normal. We then settle down to maintain the improvements we have made and console ourselves with the thought that this is the way most other Christians live. We may even have cause for pride when we see how many improvements we have compared to what we see in others.

Can you see the big mistake in all this? This old behavior pattern is the product of our fallen human nature. When we become true Christians, as we have seen, we receive a new nature; we are made partakers of the divine nature. This gives us a new source for living.

The first R taught us to Realize that in God's sight when Christ died, I died. God has finished with the old nature which is the flesh. We have become new creatures; the old things have passed away, and all things have become new.

Our old behavior pattern is the path of the old nature, the flesh. The big mistake we make is in trying to improve it. God has finished with it, but we try to make it acceptable to Him. Romans 8:8 says, "So then they that are in the flesh cannot please God," but we try to Christianize the old behavior pattern, to Christianize the flesh. This is all wrong. It may sound good to the human heart, but it does nothing for the heart of God.

This one area is the great point of failure in many Christian lives. They are sincere and love the Lord, wanting to

live for Him good, noble, pure lives. But they fail to see that
there is only one good, noble, pure Christian life, and that is
the life of Christ. Jesus said, "I am the way, the truth, and
the life." There is only one way, only one truth, and only
one life. No amount of sincere improvement to the old behavior pattern will ever make it acceptable to God.

What then is the answer? The answer is the glory of the
mystery of God's will. No human mind could ever imagine
this tremendous solution to the problem of failure in the life
of the believer. The answer is to make a new behavior pattern.

How do we proceed to make this new behavior pattern?
The answer is to put into practice the three R's of which we
have been speaking.

Let us take a practical example which is surely found in the
life of every Christian. Consider a fear, a temptation, or an
anxiety such as we meet with day by day. When such a thing
comes into our life, our immediate action is the reaction of
the old behavior pattern. We respond by being fearful, or
fighting temptation, or rationalizing worry. We try to handle
the situation ourselves. Even though we have failed many
times before, we do a rerun of the whole issue.

When I use the first R, my reaction is totally different. I
realize that in God's plan for handling the situation, I must
count myself out. I am dead, therefore I don't have to fight
this particular problem.

Then I use the second R. I act as if I was dead to the thing.
I bring the whole issue before the risen, victorious Christ who
indwells me by His Holy Spirit. I say words like these: "Lord
Jesus, this is the problem, the fear, the sin and, dear Lord,
I can do nothing about it. I'm helpless, completely incapable
of handling the situation."

We need to be honest with God in this area, to admit our
failures. Don't try to bluff God, tell Him the truth—that you
are licked.

But in the same breath in which we say, "Lord Jesus, I can't," we are quick to add, "But Lord Jesus, you can!" This very phrase can become a key to eternal blessing. "Lord Jesus, I can't, but Lord Jesus, you can!"

We follow up now by using the third R, where we yield the whole thing and ourselves to God. We respond to His call and claim His promises. We can say, "Lord Jesus, I can't but Lord Jesus, You can. So here and now I want to commit this thing to You. I don't know how You will handle the situation, but I don't need to know. I do believe that as I commit this thing to You now and keep on committing it to You, that You will give me victory Your way."

This is how Proverbs 3:6 can become a living reality in your experience: "In all thy ways acknowledge him, and he shall direct thy paths."

As I count myself out and count Christ in, acknowledging Him in all His risen power as God's answer to the power of sin in my life, then He directs my path. He does not improve the old behavior pattern. He makes new paths for me to tread. He goes with me and walks with me in the paths of His choosing.

I remember once counselling with a college man. He told me of a sin that came and filled his mind. He told how he had struggled to fight this thing but without success. We then shared the truths I have written above. I counselled him to handle this particular sin by acknowledging his failure and by making a definite commitment of the whole issue to Christ, whenever the attack should return. He came to me some days later and told me how he had been in prayer that morning when suddenly these evil thoughts had come and flooded his mind. Again he was overwhelmed with temptation, but he told me that he did not struggle this time. He had said, "Lord Jesus, this is the sin, and I can do nothing about it. Lord Jesus, I can't but you can. So here and now I commit my mind and my thoughts into your power."

He went on to add that as he continued on his knees the storm of evil desires swept in like a flood, so he kept on repeating, "Lord Jesus I can't, but Lord Jesus, you can!" After what seemed a long time the storm suddenly departed and he felt a peace he had never known before. We rejoiced in the victory of Christ, but I warned him that this was not the end of the problem. Satan would come again and again to attack him in all sorts of ways, but he had to remember the teaching of the Word of God, and learn to yield continually to Christ.

It is this continual yielding to Christ that establishes the new behavior pattern. The more I acknowledge Him, the more He will direct my paths. The more He directs my path, the more firm and true will be my new behavior pattern.

This does not mean that I will become perfect in a day, or in a lifetime. Even Paul, the greatest Christian who ever lived, said, "Not as though I had already attained, either were already perfect: but I follow after . . . I press toward the mark" (Phil 3:12, 14).

This becomes my new way of life. It will not be easy. Jesus never promised that the Christian life would be easy. It is something we have to work at day by day. It becomes a work of faith and a walk of faith.

We need to be prepared for the times of inevitable failure. There will be times when Satan will catch us unprepared. Something will suddenly arise, perhaps when we are under pressure or when we are tired or not feeling well. In an unguarded moment we will react, just as it comes naturally, and it will be the old behavior pattern once more.

As soon as we are aware that we have stepped once more into independence, we should confess this sin and seek the forgiveness and cleansing promised in 1 John 1:8, 9. And it can be a warning to us to keep close to the Lord.

As we learn to walk this way, practicing the presence of Christ, acknowledging Him in all our ways, then we reestablish the fellowship that was lost in the Garden. The more we love Him, the more we seek Him, and the sweeter will be our fellowship.

Not only do we find a great blessing this way, but the Lord Himself also can find blessing. Hebrews 12:2 says, "who for the joy that was set before him endured the cross, despising the shame." This is part of the joy that was set before Him, the restoration of the fellowship that was lost through independence. As we commit ourselves to Him, so we demonstrate our dependence, and as we do that, we show our love and trust.

One further word of counsel: do not expect a sudden and immediate transformation of your character and personality as you start to form this new behavior pattern. Remember that much of what God does, comes and grows little by little. There are no such things as instant dawn, instant spring, or instant roses. They all come gradually in varying ways as God has planned. Just as a seed grows day by day, so the truth will grow in our hearts. Little by little as the weeks and months go by, we will sense an increasing ability to commit to Christ and rest in His power.

This is called growing in grace. If we continue in our old behavior pattern, either proving it or improving it, there is no continuing work of grace in our hearts. Instead of growing in grace, we continue growing in disgrace, as we demonstrate the independence of the flesh, to our own cost and failure.

So God has a plan to deal with the penalty of sin; it is personal involvement with the death of Christ. In like manner, He has a plan to deal with the power of sin in the life of the believer; it is a personal involvement with the life of Christ. God has provided all I need, what matters now is how far I have obeyed His will and become personally involved with the risen Lord who indwells me, who will never leave me nor forsake me.

6

THE END OF REBELLION

THE MORE I READ the Bible, the more I see the faithfulness of God in all His promises. The Old Testament and the New Testament both teach this great truth in word and in illustration. Many of us, when we talk of God keeping His promises, think of all the good things He has promised. Many do exist, but we are considering in this chapter that God not only keeps His promises of peace, but also of punishment.

The history of God's people in the Old Testament is the tragic demonstration of how they never learned this lesson. Only when the blow fell were they sorry and full of repentance.

The greatest demonstration of God's hand in punishment will be seen in relation to this whole concept of rebellion about which we have been thinking. Just now the world is engaged in a runaway experience of rebellion in every area of human relationship. The pace is heating up, the areas of rebellion are increasing and widening. But someday there will come a time of reckoning and a day of judgment.

We love to comfort ourselves with such promises as Philippians 2:9-11: "Wherefore God also hath highly exalted him, and given him a name which is above every name: that at the name of Jesus every knee should bow, of things in heaven, and things in earth, and things under the earth; and that every tongue should confess that Jesus Christ is Lord, to the glory of God the Father."

This gives us joy as we consider the glory all for Christ,

and as we think of all the godless, wicked knees that will someday bow to Him. We praise God for this. This is a promise
which we greatly anticipate.

But we need to be reminded that someday each one of us,
believer and unbeliever, will meet the Lord in judgment.
We are challenged and subdued by this fact. Many Christians,
true believers, are completely ignorant of this approaching
judgment. They run around, going their own sweet way,
"doing their own thing" with never a thought to what the
Bible has to say.

I find the teaching of the Word in this area can be used to
pull us up sharply and awaken us to our responsibility. There
is no doubt that if all believers were aware of the truth concerning judgment, then our churches would be places of
power, witnessing would be a constant occupation, and mis-
sions would achieve their greatest impact.

So let us turn to God's Word and find the Lord Jesus, not
now as Saviour, but as Judge.

First look with me in Revelation 20:7-15. This passage
begins by detailing the last demonstration of rebellion by the
person of Satan. As well as being the last, it is also the greatest as far as numbers and involvement of nations is concerned.
Verse 9 tells of the tremendous physical victory from the
hand of God. Then verse 10 speaks of the final judgment on
Satan. That which began in Isaiah 14 finds its final fulfillment here: "And the devil that deceived them was cast into
the lake of fire and brimstone, where the beast and the false
prophet are, and shall be tormented day and night for ever
and ever."

Whatever this means we do not know, and we do not need
to know, except to realize that God keeps His promises of
peace and punishment.

Verse 11 then speaks of a great white throne. This is the
throne of judgment and the one who sits there is Christ. We
know this because Jesus said in John 5:22, "For the Father

judgeth no man, but hath committed all judgment unto the Son."

The following verses then tell us who are the ones who will appear there for judgment. Verse 12 says, "And I saw the dead, small and great, stand before God." In three other places following this they are called "the dead." From this we can learn that there will be no true believers there. Ephesians 2:1 tells us: "And you hath he quickened [or made alive], who were dead in trespasses and sins." Once we were dead but by the grace of God we were born again, we received life, and we became living ones.

Verse 12 gives more details: "And the books were opened: and another book was opened, which is the book of life: and the dead were judged out of those things which were written in the books, according to their works." Notice here the books of the dead, and the Book of the living ones. There are many books of the dead; there is only one Book of Life. This last Book is mentioned in five places in the Bible; it is the Lamb's Book of Life. It contains the names of all those who belong to Him. Everyone's name is in a book, either in the books of the dead or in the one Book of Life.

The Book of Life is at the great white throne to serve as a check on those who are being judged. You will see in verse 15 that the punishment came not to those who were in the books of the dead, but to those who were not in the Book of Life.

We have considered this passage to make sure of one fact: no true believer will ever be there. If you know Christ as your Saviour you will never appear before the judgment at the great white throne. Conversely, if these words are being read by someone who is not sure that his name is in the Lamb's Book of Life, the wisest thing you can do is to come with your need to the Saviour at this moment. Don't wait to meet Him as your Judge.

There is another place of judgment and to this one all believers will be summoned. This time it is to deal with the issue of rebellion in the life of the Christian.

We can see this in 2 Corinthians 5:9-11 "Wherefore we labour, that, whether present or absent, we may be accepted of him. For we must all appear before the judgment seat of Christ; that every one may receive the things done in his body, according to that he hath done, whether good or bad. Knowing therefore the terror of the Lord, we persuade men."

These words are very challenging! See those four words in verse 10: "we must all appear." Notice the word "all"; no one will be left out. The word "must" tells us that we have no choice; we must be there. It goes on to say, "that every one may receive the things done in his body." Although all of us will be there, we appear one at a time. This is not a mass movement, or a church judgment, or even a family appearance, it is a personal thing. "Everyone . . . his body."

Paul's words in verse 16 are very revealing: "Knowing therefore the terror of the Lord." This in no way depicts Paul as a cringing coward. The Amplified New Testament says, "Therefore, being conscious of fearing the Lord with respect and reverence." Paul had a wholesome respect for the holiness and majesty of God. He knew he had to answer for his life lived here on earth, and such knowledge brought awe and reverence to his heart. This thought of the holiness of God is one of the missing ingredients in many Christian lives today. A world which has lost respect for the dignity of human life can so affect the lives of Christians that they begin to lose respect all along the line. It is so easy to see Jesus as our brother and God as a friendly neighbor.

The Holy Spirit draws our attention to the same thought in Romans 14:10: "For we shall all stand before the judgment seat of Christ." Notice again "we shall all."

This use of the phrase "the judgment seat of Christ" in both these passages is very significant. To the people of the early church the meaning was clear. It reminded them of what often happened. A certain lord, prince, or rich man would leave his possessions and go to visit another area. During his absence he would leave his servants with their various jobs to do. On his return he would have a checkup on what went on during his absence. This is exactly what a business executive would do today. It is a test and a check to see the response of the assistants in order to discover what had been accomplished. The Lord Jesus Himself used such an illustration in His parables.

In the culture of those early days the lord sat on a seat with a table before him. On the table were the records of the schedules given and fulfilled. He then discussed with each member of his group the work done, commenting as necessary. This is what the judgment seat was—a place of scrutiny and examination.

With this information we can now get a picture of what has been told us: "We must all appear before the judgment seat of Christ; that every one may receive." You will be there; I will be there. Someone may comment that such a gathering of all the believers who ever lived would take a long, long time to finish. The answer to such a remark is that time will have ceased to exist when this is being fulfilled.

We can find more information as to what happens at this judgment seat by turning to 1 Corinthians 3:9-16, which introduces the idea that we are laborers together with God. The end of verse 10 says, "But let every man take heed how he buildeth thereupon."

From verse 12 the message continues as follows:

> Now if any man build upon this foundation gold, silver, precious stones, wood, hay, stubble;
> Every man's work shall be made manifest: for the day shall declare it, because it shall be revealed by fire; and the fire shall try every man's work of what sort it is.
> If any man's work abide which he hath built thereupon, he shall receive a reward.

> If any man's work shall be burned, he shall suffer loss:
> but he himself shall be saved; yet so as by fire.
> Know ye not that ye are the temple of God, and that the
> Spirit of God dwelleth in you? (1 Co 3:12-16).

This is a tremendous passage and it has much to say to each one of us, especially as we face up to our own rebellion as Christians and the many times we walk in independence.

We have already seen that there will be no believers at the great white throne, but that every Christian will stand before Christ at the judgment seat. Now, let us make sure of one very important fact. There are some Christians who become very apprehensive when they consider this judgment, because they have the idea that there is a possibility they may never get to heaven after all. Somehow they wonder whether they will really make it.

We do need to view this judgment with awe and wonder just as we saw Paul did in 2 Corinthians 5:11, but not for the reason stated above.

The Bible is here teaching what actually is the object coming up for judgment. See for yourself the repeated use of the words "every man's work." This comes twice in verse 13 and once each in verses 14 and 15. It is not the man who is being judged, but his works.

See how personal this occasion is. Just as we saw the use of the words *every one* in 2 Corinthians 5:10, so we have the singular emphasis in verse 10, "every man"; verse 12, "any man"; verse 13, "every man's," "every man's"; verse 14, "any man's . . . he"; verse 15, "any man's . . . he." There is no sense of hurry. The Lord will have time for every man and woman.

When we put these two considerations together we can see now the whole point of the judgment. This is no question of whether we will get to heaven, the very judgment itself is held in heaven. Anyone who reaches this time of searching before the Lord has already an assurance of his home in heaven.

The whole process of examination is directed towards the life we have lived here on earth and the works we have accomplished. The very mention of the word *works* is misleading to some people. This is not a question of being saved by our works. The Bible teaches quite plainly and repeatedly that we are saved by the blood of Christ and by no merits of our own. These are not works for salvation, but works following salvation.

What is the basis of this judgment? What standards are to be used? We can find the answer to this in the last five words of verse 13: "of what sort it is." This is one of the most significant phrases in the whole passage. Notice the basis for scrutiny is not how much it is, but "what sort it is."

These are very comforting and challenging words. We might have the idea that when we come before the Lord, we do so with our accumulated wealth of good works. If this were so, we can easily see how certain people would have enormous piles of good deeds. Just think for a moment of the tremendous results from the lives of people such as Billy Graham, D. L. Moody, John Wesley, and other great preachers down through the ages. These men would stand there overshadowed by the mountainous accumulation of their good works.

On the other hand, there would be many little nobodies whose lives had not seen such an abundance of blessing. Just think of some of the bedridden, who never have an opportunity to get out and about. How pitiful would be their tiny handful compared with the giants of the faith.

This would be the situation if the judgment were based on how much it is. Thank God, His standard is "what sort it is."

At this point, the value of God's wonderful will and plan for us begins to take a new shape. Remember, the mystery of God's will was that we should be made partakers of the divine nature. We already had, and still possess, our old fallen human nature; but when we were born again, we received

a new nature. The old nature is the rebel, always wanting
its own way, whether good or bad. When Adam stepped into
independence, he took all humanity with him. This is the
tragedy of a world in rebellion. Human nature, the flesh, has
always continued to walk in independence. It knows no other
way; it cannot change its inherent nature. This was why God
finished with the flesh and gave to us the very life of Christ
Himself.

Now can you see why the whole basis of the judgment is "of
what sort it is"? There are only two sorts of works, *my* sort
and *His* sort.

My sort is the result of my own deliberate choosing. I
planned, I schemed, and this is what happened—whether it is
good, bad, or indifferent. Every one of these works was done
in independence, as I thought I knew how I could behave
or choose. My sort is the proof of my own independence and
rebellion, not to my credit but to my condemnation!

His sort is the outcome of a life totally yielded to Him. It
is His choice. His plan performed by His power for His
glory. When it is my sort I get the glory, however much I
protest otherwise. If my protests are loud enough, I even get
the added glory of being thought humble! Not so in the life
that is yielded to Christ.

It is fascinating to see the life of Christ on earth as the
perfect example of a constant, unfailing, dependent life. In
John 5:19 He said, "Verily, verily, I say unto you, The Son
can do nothing of himself, but what he seeth the Father do."
In verse 30 of the same chapter He added, "I can of mine own
self do nothing . . . I seek not mine own will, but the will of
the Father which hath sent me." In John 7:16 we read, "Jesus
answered them, and said, My doctrine is not mine, but his
that sent me." John 8:28 brings this added thought: "I do
nothing of myself; but as my Father hath taught me, I speak
these things." John 14:10 has a challenging word for us in
this very connection: "The words that I speak unto you I

speak not of myself: but the Father that dwelleth in me, he doeth the works."

In all these passages Jesus is demonstrating His total dependence on the One who sent Him. He claimed no credit or honor for anything. Though He was the Son of God, He never used His divine power for His own ends or for His own glory. The Father who sent Him was the source and continuing supply of His plans and power.

This brings into special focus the words of our Lord in John 20:21: "As my Father hath sent me, even so send I you." The Father sent Jesus to walk in total dependence. The first Adam was created to walk in dependence upon God, but he stepped into independence. Now see the significance of 1 Corinthians 15:45, "the last Adam was made a quickening spirit." Jesus was the last Adam, the One who never failed. He demonstrated, as we have seen, His total dependence upon the One who sent Him.

This is the significance of the words, "as My Father hath sent me, even so send I you." He is the One who sends us and He wants us to walk even as He walked. He wants us to walk dependent on Him. When this comes true in our daily experience, then our works become His sort, just as His works were the Father's sort.

To enable us to achieve this quality of life, "the last Adam was made a quickening spirit." He was a life-giving Spirit. He sent His Holy Spirit to indwell us, so that we might be partakers of the divine nature. As we yield to Him by our new behavior pattern, then what is seen in our lives is not "our sort" but "His sort." Just as Jesus could say, "The Father that dwelleth in me, he doeth the works," we should seek to live so that, as much as possible, we can say, "The Saviour who dwells in me, He is doing the works." Remember, the only way this can ever be true is as we seek to make the new behavior pattern: "Lord Jesus, I can't . . . but Lord Jesus, you can!"

This idea of the two sorts is graphically illustrated in verse 12 of 1 Corinthians 3: "Now if any man build upon this foundation gold, silver, precious stones, wood, hay, stubble." These six separate items are used to set forth what the works are; they picture for us in parable language what our works will be at the judgment seat. Notice that there are two sorts of works. These six items fall into two groups: one consisting of gold, silver, and precious stones; the other group comprised of wood, hay, and stubble.

It is easy to recognize which group represents His sort, which has come through the outworking of the indwelling Spirit; it is the gold, silver and the precious stones. Incidentally, these three items were a figure of Christ in the Old Testament, in the temple construction, in the redemption process, and in many other ways.

Likewise, it is easy to see which group represents our sort, the product of a rebellious human nature which is dead in the sight of God. The very items themselves—wood, hay, stubble—are dead things. Once they had life, just as Adam had life; but now they are dead, just as human nature is dead in the sight of God.

This then is the basis for judgment: "of what sort it is." The Bible uses vivid symbolism to show how the actual test is made: "The fire shall try every man's work." Imagine fire being applied to the six items mentioned above. Nothing would happen to the gold, silver, and precious stones. They would stand firm for one special reason. When gold is made, it lives in fire to burn off the dross. Silver is made by a process we read of in Psalm 12:6: "As silver tried in a furnace of fire, purified seven times." Precious stones are the product of fire and pressure operating below the earth's surface. No fire would harm these three, because they have already passed through the fire.

But think of the effect on the three dead things, the wood, hay, and stubble. There would be a rush of flame, a roar of fire, and when the testing was finished, all that remained would be a heap of ashes. Nothing left but the ashes of sorrow and regret. If this is a picture of your life now—ashes of regret—consider the promise of Isaiah 61:3. Jesus, in Luke 4:18-19, said that these words applied to Him. Therefore He is able "to give them beauty for ashes." There is still time to have the beauty of Christ seen through our yielded lives to cancel out the ashes of human failure.

All these words are written in the Bible to make us aware that some day there will come a time of reckoning for each believer. If every Christian really believed this teaching and faced up to the stark fact that one day he will actually stand before Christ, what a lot of rethinking and reevaluating there would be.

But this isn't the end of the story of the judgment seat. One remarkable fact emerges from verse 14: "If any man's work abide . . . he shall receive a reward." This is an embarrassing thought in one way. Many of us might respond by saying, "But I don't want any reward. Just to be in heaven will be enough for me." It may be enough for us, but it is not enough for the Lord! Check and see what He says in Revelation 22:12: "Behold, I come quickly; and my reward is with me, to give every man according as his work shall be." Notice here the same thought as we have already seen—"every man," "his work," "my reward."

What these rewards are, we have no idea. Several guesses have been made, but the actual truth is still one of God's unrevealed secrets. It is good that this is so, otherwise we may be tempted to glorify the reward instead of giving all the glory to the Redeemer.

Still speaking of rewards, verse 15 adds, "If any man's work shall be burned, he shall suffer loss: but he himself shall be saved; yet so as by fire." The purpose of the judgment seat is for the giving and the withholding of rewards. Notice that if there is no reward, even then the Christian is saved, yet so as by fire.

In these six chapters we have had a long look at rebellion as we see it today, both in the world around us and especially in our own hearts. The whole purpose of Christian witnessing is to proclaim to a lost, dead, rebellious world that God has an answer in Christ. But before we get out to tell others, there needs to be a reckoning up in our own lives.

We may be saved, be born again, and rejoicing in the hope of a home in heaven. But the crucial question is this: what is my relationship to the risen, victorious, indwelling Christ? Am I still walking in independence, even under the disguise of enthusiastic service—*my* enthusiasm—*my* service? Am I still struggling and fighting to live the Christian life, bewildered by my fears and sick of my failure?

There is an answer. In these chapters we have shared together all that Christ can be day by day. May I suggest that this may be your need at this time. You have found Jesus as the sin-bearer at the cross. Have you gone on to find Him the burden-bearer in the crisis, and the source of all your power?

Prayer of Realization

O God my Father, I thank you for all that I have learned by the guiding of your Holy Spirit.

I recognize the truth of rebellion; I see it all around me. I see it and know it within my own heart. I acknowledge my sin and my rebellion.

At this time I would come into a fuller realization of all that Jesus Christ is.

I thank you for His sacrificial death. I adore and worship Him because through His death I can be saved from my sins.

Now I bow in wonder, realizing the power of His saving life as He indwells me by His Holy Spirit.

Lord Jesus, this opens to me a totally new way of life. So

far I have been confined to the failure of my old behavior pattern, shut into myself and my own resources.

Dear Lord, I see now that as I live this way, I am walking in independence, perpetuating the rebellion that is the curse of this world.

I see now my need to bring in a new behavior pattern based solely on who You are and what You can be in my life day by day.

As I realize this, help me to grow in grace, counting only on Your presence, committing all to Your power.

In doing this I would prepare myself for that day when I see You face to face. Help me to walk in awe as I look only to You. May Your gold, silver and precious stones be seen more and more in my daily life as the life of Christ is made manifest in my mortal flesh.

Do all this for the honor and glory of Your holy name, for the blessing of others through my yielded life, and for the sake of my blessed Lord and Saviour Jesus Christ. Amen.

PART II

ILLUSTRATIONS OF THIS TRUTH

7

THE HEROES WHO FAILED

IN THE FIRST PART of this book we have been concerned with the truth concerning the rebellion in the world today. We have seen how, and where the rebellion began. We have seen how and why God has provided the complete answer to the results of sin and rebellion in the heart of man. We have made the study practical and shown how we ourselves can be involved in a living way with the fulness of Christ.

In this second part I want us to look into some of the stories in the Old Testament to find illustrations of the very situations we have been considering. I have been encouraged these last few years, as I have dug into the Old Testament, to see the tremendous message it has for today. Far from being an old-fashioned book, it is amazingly relevant to today's situations and needs.

We will see ourselves portrayed in many areas of failure and misjudgment as we look at men and women like ourselves moving into situations brought about by their own rebellious choice.

The Bible tells us to examine their motives and measure their failures for one express purpose: that we may learn from them and allow the Spirit to guide us into His own ways.

I have seen again and again how the Spirit has taken an Old Testament story and through its message He has spoken with real convicting power. The Spirit of God uses the Word of God in a unique way. There is an anointing on the written

Word that has power to break through to the tough heart, the confused mind, the careless life, and even to the antagonistic personality. My prayer is that what God has done many times before, He will be pleased to do once more—through His own Word, for His own glory.

Our first story will be found in several books, as we build up the continuity, but we can make a start by looking at the third to the last book in the Old Testament, the book of Haggai, chapter 1 and verses 5-7: "Now therefore thus saith the LORD of Hosts; Consider your ways. Ye have sown much, and bring in little; ye eat, but ye have not enough; ye drink, but ye are not filled with drink; ye clothe you, but there is none warm; and he that earneth wages earneth wages to put it into a bag with holes. Thus saith the Lord of hosts; Consider your ways."

This is straight talk from the mouth of God, an analysis of failure. People doing all the right things, but getting all the wrong answers. The words were applied to a special group of people, as we shall see in a moment. But the point to consider is that these words are eternal truth; this is what happens to all God's people when certain things happen. Verse 6 could be a vivid description of some churches today. I have come across churches where the gospel is faithfully proclaimed, where there is no false teaching, but these same words could be written across the whole church program. Much sowing but little reaping, much "eating" but no satisfaction, plenty of activities and a sound financial position—but a sense of bankruptcy over all the work.

This is why the message we are considering in these next few chapters is so vital to the present-day church. Remember that when God does a diagnosis of a spiritual disease, He always gives the correct prescription for a cure.

Not only is this true of some churches, it is more true of many Christians. I meet such fine people. There is plenty of activity, but no productivity; plenty of going, but no arriving;

much hunger, but no satisfaction; having a spiritual thirst but never able to quench the dryness.

To all such the Lord still says, "Consider your ways."

Who were these people in Haggai who presented such a discouraging picture? The sad and strange thing is that they were a group of heroes. We will see what wonderful people they were, great in character and noble in courage, and yet in the most pitiful condition.

The story begins back in the book of 2 Chronicles. This book contains thirty-six chapters and tells the unfolding story of the kings of Judah. It is essentially a countdown to destruction. It shows the increasing spiritual and social sin of the nation. It recounts how God sent prophets to warn the people of the consequences of their continued sin. We see and hear prophets pleading with the people to forsake their idols and to get right with God.

Then the pace quickened. Idolatry increased. God's word became more threatening. The people were told that if they continue in their rebellious ways, then the Lord will destroy His holy temple and obliterate Jerusalem as a city. To this they responded with foolish incredulity. They said, "God would never do such a thing. Destroy His own temple— never! Destroy Jerusalem—never!"

The tragedy was they thought they could sin and get away with it. Just as today some people say, "God would never destroy America. It is God's own country. He would never allow it to happen!"

They counted on the love of God, but forgot the holiness of God and the eternal faithfulness of His promises for not only peace but also punishment.

Thus it is we come to chapter 36, the end of the story. When this chapter begins, there were still twenty-two and a half years left before the blow is to fall, but no one cared. The years passed by. Twenty-two, twenty-one, twenty—until there were eleven years left on the clock of grace.

The last king to reign was Zedekiah. He was twenty-one years old and as heedless as the rest. Verse 12 recounts that "he . . . humbled not himself before Jeremiah the prophet speaking from the mouth of God." Where sin had abounded, it did much more abound. Verse 14 records, "Moreover all the chief of the priests, and the people, transgressed very much after all the abominations of the heathen; and polluted the house of God which he had allowed in Jerusalem."

The wonderful thing is to see the reaction of God to this ugly and evil situation. Verse 15 tells that God continued to send His messengers to them "because he had compassion on his people, and on his dwelling place." What an amazing contrast, the contempt of the people and the compassion of God.

But the years ticked by relentlessly, as verse 16 recounts, "they mocked the messengers of God, and despised his words, and misused his prophets, until the wrath of the LORD arose against the people, till there was no remedy." What awful words—"till there was no remedy"!

They had rebelled, gone their own way, walked in complete independence—and then the blow fell. All that God said and promised came true. Jerusalem was destroyed, the walls were demolished; worst of all, the beautiful, glittering holy temple was burned, along with every other consumable building. There was a fearful slaughter of the inhabitants, and the survivors were taken away to Babylon. When the final curtain fell, Jerusalem was nothing but a heap of chaotic rubble and burned-out buildings.

God had said what He meant, and He meant what He said —but they learned their lesson too late!

The ruin that had been Jerusalem remained uncared for and neglected for seventy years. Stop a moment, and get a good picture of how Jerusalem might have looked at the end of those seventy forgotten years. Think of the initial chaotic ruin, then see it covered with the weeds and trees and bushes of seventy years growth. The chances are it would have been almost unrecognizable. The wasted years of rebellious living had produced a wasted place of ruin and tragedy.

But that was not the end of the story so far as God was concerned. God had His plans all ready for a new start. Just as He had prophesied, so it came to pass.

At the end of the seventy years, God moved the heart of King Cyrus to proclaim a message to all the Jews in his kingdom.

The book of Ezra, which follows the final chapter of 2 Chronicles, repeats God's challenge almost word for word. Almost as if the Lord had the end and the beginning in His hands.

We read in Ezra 1:2, 3 these thrilling words: "Thus saith Cyrus king of Persia, The LORD God of heaven hath given me all the kingdoms of the earth; and he hath charged me to build him an house at Jerusalem, which is in Judah. Who is there among you of all his people? his God be with him, and let him go up to Jerusalem, which is in Judah, and build the house of the LORD God of Israel." This was the dawn of a new day, a beginning for God and His people.

Notice carefully what the call was for: "to build him an house at Jerusalem, which is in Judah." God asked for one thing only, volunteers who would be willing to leave all and build a house for God. Incidentally, see the pathetic way in which the Word says "Jerusalem, which is in Judah." Directions were needed to pinpoint a place which no longer existed on the map of human history.

This message of Cyrus was blazed throughout his great kingdom. Every Jewish synagogue might have had the message read out for the ears of all the people attending. It perhaps became the one topic of conversation for all Jews. The more they heard it, the more their hearts would be searched.

Psalm 137 tells us the kind of song they sang during the seventy wasted years: "By the rivers of Babylon, there we sat down, yea, we wept, when we remembered Zion . . . How shall we sing the LORD's song in a strange land? . . . If I forget thee, O Jerusalem . . . If I do not remember thee . . . if I prefer not Jerusalem above my chief joy." This is what they sang; now what would they do? Singing nostalgic words to plaintive music is one thing; leaving all and stepping out for God is another.

The pages of all history record the amazing capacity of the Jews to rise from the depths of utter poverty to wealth and abundance. This is especially true of the land of Israel today. No one who has been there will ever forget the miracle of rebirth which can be seen in so many places. God has given His people a unique capacity to succeed in business, especially in the world of high finance.

This has ever been so; Joseph in Egypt is an outstanding example. It was so in the day of Cyrus. Seventy years before, the people of Jerusalem had struggled their weary way across the desert to stumble finally into a strange land, captives of the conqueror Nebuchadnezzar.

But that was seventy years ago! Over two generations had passed, and Jewish children were born who had never seen Jerusalem. Anyone remembering Jerusalem was well over seventy years old. Following the pattern of their unique ability to rise and prosper, there now were many Jews living in affluence. Babylon had much to offer in the way of sumptuous living if you had the right kind of money.

Thus it was that the challenge of God through Cyrus came to a people at ease and at peace. Most of them had never seen Jerusalem. They had sung nostalgic songs as they rested at ease in their lovely homes; but singing sad songs in the cool shade and slogging it out over miles of hot dusty sand are two different things.

Try and recapture what God was asking, and what was entailed in that one word *obedience*. It meant foot slogging for five months over wilderness country. It meant arriving at a site which would be almost unrecognizable because of the years of growth covering the area. Then there would be many months of "blood, toil, tears, and sweat" as they cleared the site, uprooting scrub, bushes, and tearing out trees. Remember, all this had to be done with bare hands; there were no tractors, bulldozers, or earth-moving machinery. There were no stores to which they could go to replace broken tools, no cool drinks at the local drug store. Just work, work, and more work! And they could not catch a quick jet back to Babylon; it was a once-for-all decision, a one-way trip!

Put yourself in the sandals of one of these successful Jewish businessmen in Babylon. Count the cost. Think of your wife and family—no schools for the children! No future but the hard grind of sweating and building. What would you have done? Would you have gone, or would you have found a thousand good reasons for staying in Babylon and promoting prayer groups for those dear missionaries in Jerusalem?

I want us to see the caliber of the people who made that great decision. They were not just enthusiastic supporters of a church program. They had counted the cost. They were sacrificing their family and their fortune down to the last shekel. They meant business. They were one of the finest groups of heroes ever to appear in the pages of Jewish history. We salute their courage, their devotion, their love to God. We see in them a challenge to our own hearts.

And yet these are the same people we met in Haggai, chapter 1, when our story began. Impossible, you say! How could it be? That is why we are studying their experiences, so that we can learn a deep lesson. They were heroes, yes; but they failed.

But before we finish this chapter, let us see the heroes in action, in all the glory of sweat and suffering. Turn to Ezra 2 and there you will see the roll of honor. Here we have detailed for us the numbers of those who stepped out for God, and the places from which they came. They are listed in family groups. Some of the groups were large, such as the

2,056 who came with the man, appropriately named Bigvai, verse 14. Others were much smaller, such as the party of 42 who came with Azmaveth, verse 24. But every one was a hero for God.

Verse 64 tells us the whole group numbered 42,360. We find from verse 65 that there were 7,337 servants; so they must have been people of some substance to possess so many servants. An interesting comment in the same verse is that they had a mixed choir of two hundred. They took their music with them!

Verses 66 and 67 tell how many animals they possessed, 8,136 all told. From this we can see that many people walked on foot. They surely meant business.

A very sad and revealing incident comes to light in verse 59. When these heroes finally made it to Jerusalem they reported in by families to the official in charge of party membership. He had a book containing the list of true Jewish families, and as each one came and gave his name, he ticked him off the list.

One group came to him, "but they could not show their father's house, and their seed, whether they were of Israel." What a shock for these people! They had just finished the long journey only to find out that they did not belong. They looked like Jews, behaved like Jews, and they had made the same wearisome trip: only to discover that they were not eligible. They did not belong!

In Matthew 7:22-23 we have a prophecy from the lips of the Lord Jesus which describes a similar situation: "Many will say to me in that day, Lord, Lord, have we not prophesied in thy name? and in thy name have cast out devils? and in thy name done many wonderful works? And then will I profess unto them, I never knew you: depart from me, ye that work iniquity."

These people in Jesus' story also thought they belonged to Him because of what they did and where they went. Notice

His terrible comment: "I never knew you." Not that Jesus had forgotten them; He never knew them. In John 10:27-28 Jesus said: "My sheep hear my voice, and I know them, and they follow me: And I give unto them eternal life."

This group who arrived at Jerusalem, only to be rejected, were also heroes; but they also failed because they did not belong.

There may be some one reading these words and this may be your case. You may look like a true Christian, behave like a Christian, go where Christians go, do what Christians do. That alone isn't enough. Do you belong? Does Jesus know you personally?

8
WHY BUILD A TEMPLE?

BEFORE WE GO ON to find out why these heroes failed, there is one matter we need to discuss and really understand: why build a temple? What was so very important about making the temple the one and only reason for the long journey from Babylon to Jerusalem?

Today we might consider many things more important: schools, hospitals, and houses, just to mention three. The Jews have been back in Israel since 1948, but they have not built a temple. They have had massive building programs of places necessary for industry, agriculture, education, and culture—but no temple.

In order to understand the full implications of the story in Haggai we need to know the supreme and unique importance of the temple in that day. In order to understand the real meaning of the Christian faith, with all the possibilities for power and peace, we also need to understand and know the reason for building a temple. Let us turn to the Bible and see for ourselves its importance in the economy of God.

We turn first to Exodus 25. By the time we reach this part of the story of God's dealings with His people, many things have happened. The people have been freed from the bondage of Egypt. Moses has been used by God to discipline Pharaoh and deliver the people. They have crossed the Red Sea and seen Egypt's army perish in its waters. Operation Deliverance has been completed, and now Moses was preparing for further experiences with God. All the wilderness journey with its unknown, unexpected forty years of wandering lay ahead.

It was at this time that God did something new in the sight of Moses. He told Moses to "speak unto the children of Israel, that they bring me an offering" (v. 2). God then detailed the items needed, and Moses was told why the offering was requested: "And let them make me a sanctuary; that I may dwell among them" (v. 8).

This sanctuary was to be known as the tabernacle. It was to last for many years, right up to the days of Solomon.

The important thing here is to see why God wanted this tabernacle or tent erected: "That I may dwell among them." Just consider the tremendous implications of this desire of God. God's first thought for a redeemed people was that He might dwell among them. There was no question of waiting until they became more cultured and attractive.

At that time there were over a million people, many of whom had been downtrodden slaves. They were uncultured, unwashed, and unlovely. They would go on to murmur, complain, and test the patience and love of God time and time again. But even so, knowing all this, it was still the first desire of God to dwell in the midst of His people.

The chapters following this request tell how God instructed Moses as to the details of the tabernacle. Then in Exodus 29:45-46 we hear these words from God: "And I will dwell among the children of Israel, and will be their God. And they shall know that I am the LORD their God, that brought them forth out of the land of Egypt, that I may dwell among them: I am the LORD their God."

Notice this specific affirmation from the lips of God: "I brought them forth . . . that I may dwell among them." Again we see the initial thought repeated; the purpose of the tabernacle was that God might dwell there.

The remainder of Exodus gives continuing details of the construction and use of this tabernacle. By the end of chapter

39 we read, "And Moses did look upon all the work, and, behold, they had done it even as the Lord had commanded, even so had they done it: and Moses blessed them."

Thus the various separate items of the tent structure were completed. God then instructed Moses to assemble and erect the various parts and so present to the Lord the finished tabernacle. God had said that if they did as He commanded, then He would come and dwell in the tabernacle. It must have been an exciting and awe-inspiring day when Moses complied with the will of God. The people assembled in their thousands to see if God meant what He had said, watching with wonder and fearful expectancy.

This is how the final moments are described in chapter 40: "So Moses finished the work. Then a cloud covered the tent of the congregation, and the glory of the Lord filled the tabernacle" (vv. 33-34). The story goes on to tell that Moses was not able to enter because of the cloud and the glory.

The book of Exodus ends by telling about the cloud by day and the fire by night which the Lord used. The cloud was there to control. When the cloud moved, they moved. When the cloud of glory rested, there was the tabernacle erected.

See now the lovely thought in the heart of God. The cloud was always there by day, the fire by night. God was always there; He would never leave them nor forsake them. As the years went by, any man or woman whose heart was worried or fearful had only to go outside his tent and look towards the tabernacle. Even on the darkest night he could see the fire of God keeping watch over His people.

So the book of Exodus begins with the people in bondage and ends with the same people in blessing. At the commencement, Pharaoh was in control; at the close, God is in control.

This was the way God dwelt among his people right up to the days of David. Then something new came into view; David had plans for a temple, a permanent building. From the outside the tabernacle was most unimpressive, just a dull-colored tent surrounded by a fence of curtains. Inside, it was aglow with the warm light of the oil lamps reflecting on the gold, but no one saw that except the priests.

The temple, on the other hand, was to be a permanent building. It was to be glorious both within and without. In 1 Chronicles 28 we read the story of David giving instructions to his son Solomon in the sight of all Israel: "Take heed now; for the LORD hath chosen thee to build an house for a sanctuary: be strong, and do it. Then David gave to Solomon his son the pattern . . . pattern of all that he had by the spirit" (vv. 10-12).

Verse 19 adds, "All this, said David, the LORD made me understand in writing by his hand upon me, even all the works of this pattern."

So once again, the plan for the house of God came from the mind of God, even as in Moses' time.

The story of how Solomon built the house of the Lord begins in 2 Chronicles 2. Chapters 3 and 4 are full of the glory, the beauty, and riches that went into the construction. We read of gold, perfect gold, and pure gold—there were even degrees of perfection! (4:21-22).

Then came the great day that was to mark the completion of this glorious temple, the house of God. As the final act, the priests carried in the ark of God with the golden cherubim above it overshadowing the mercy seat. Chapter 5 details this last exciting day. There was a tremendous choir of several thousand men, all dressed in white linen. There was a full orchestra of cymbals, psalteries, and harps. The most startling contribution came from 120 trumpeters—what an amazing volume of sound must have come from these men!

This is how the vital moment is described in verses 13 and 14:

> It came even to pass, as the trumpeters and singers were
> as one, to make one sound to be heard in praising and

thanking the LORD; and when they lifted up their voices with the trumpets and cymbals and instruments of music, and praised the LORD, saying, For he is good; and his mercy endureth for ever: that then the house was filled with the cloud, even the house of the LORD; so that the priests could not stand to minister by reason of the cloud: for the glory of the LORD had filled the house of God!

What a fantastic moment this must have been—every voice, every trumpet and instrument sounding as one! What a majestic outpouring of sound. Then, suddenly, there it was! The glory of the Lord had filled His holy temple. God had been faithful to His promise and to His people.

Then there follow some precious words. God appeared to Solomon the second time and, speaking in connection with the same temple, He said: "I have hallowed this house, which thou hast built, to put my name there for ever; and mine eyes and mine heart shall be there perpetually" (1 Kings 9:3).

Understand the glorious implications of God's promise: My name, My eyes, My heart—forever, perpetually. This was what the temple was going to become, the place where God was—His name, His eyes, His heart. His name means "all that He is" and is not merely the spelling of the letters for Jehovah. Proverbs 18:10 tells us: "The name of the LORD is a strong tower: the righteous runneth into it, and is safe." Both in the Old and New Testaments the references to the name of God or of Jesus have this same teaching: "all that He is."

So there was God's name with all His power. Then there were His eyes to see with, to search and protect His people from their enemies. Lastly, His heart, to love His people and to care for them. "Like as a father pitieth his children, so the LORD pitieth [or loves] them that fear him." (Ps 103:13).

See now the tremendous importance first of the tabernacle and then of the temple. They each served as the house of God.

God requested it and promised His own presence and power when the plan was carried out.

We began this chapter by asking, why build a temple? We can see now that this was far more important than any other building devised by men. Man's buildings may be excellent, providing shelter, comfort, education, or culture. But when God's house was built at God's request according to His plan, the whole world was changed, as God became real.

I think the most thrilling part of this study on the temple comes now as we turn to 1 Corinthians 6:19, 20 and see the very same truth spelled out in terms of our own lives: "What? know ye not that your body is the temple of the Holy Ghost which is in you, which ye have of God, and ye are not your own? For ye are bought with a price: therefore glorify God in your body, and in your spirit, which are God's."

God's first thought for His people, redeemed by the blood of the Lamb, was that He might dwell in their midst. We saw this in Exodus 25 and 29. This has never changed. When we are redeemed at the cross by the blood of Christ, the Lamb of God, then Jesus comes to indwell us in the person of His Holy Spirit. Then we become, each one of us, a temple of the Holy Spirit.

To whom did the tabernacle belong? Obviously to God, because the people brought their offerings to God, and out of their gifts was fashioned the tabernacle. So the tabernacle belonged to God.

In just the same way, the temple of Solomon belonged to God. Again it was the gifts of God's people that made the temple possible.

That is why verse 19 in 1 Corinthians 6 says, "ye are not your own." You, too, are God's temple and you belong to God. Verse 20 gives a second reason why you are not your own: you have been bought with a price, the life of the spotless Son of God.

This thought should challenge some of us as to who owns our life. Are we a temple or a trash can?

Psalm 12 has some very pertinent things to say in this connection. It begins by saying, "Help, LORD; for the godly man ceaseth; for the faithful fail from among the children of men." It is talking of what we can see in many places today, the ceasing of the godly and the failing of the faithful. These are not sinners in all their evil ways, these are believers in trouble. Verse 4 tells you why this miserable state of affairs has developed: "Who have said, With our tongue will we prevail; our lips are our own: who is lord over us?"

There are many believers who say the same things, either in thought, word, or deed, "Our lips are our own, our lives are our own, who is lord over us?" No wonder there are so many useless, defeated lives.

But as well as this thought of ownership by God, there is the lovely thought of His name, His eyes, and His heart. All that God was to them by the cloud and the fire, Jesus is much more to us by His own indwelling presence. God used the words *for ever* and *perpetually* in describing His presence to Solomon. Jesus said, "Lo, I am with you alway, even unto the end of the world" (Matthew 28:20).

The history of the children of Israel as told in the Old Testament was basically their relationship to the presence of the Lord in His tabernacle or His temple. In like manner, the success or failure of the Christian depends upon one thing only: his relationship to the indwelling Christ, the One who makes his body a temple for God.

When the people turned to God from their idols and their failure, they found Him waiting with forgiveness and cleansing and then the outpouring of His power. This is what the Lord promised them, and this is what the Lord promises us today. As we turn from our own way, from the old behavior pattern, and seek by childlike faith to be dependent on a

Christ who is there, then we, too, can move into an upward surge of joy and blessing.

The making of the new behavior pattern, as we saw it in chapter 5, is a day by day recognition of the indwelling Christ. It is reestablishing our dependence on Him and turning our backs on the rebellion of the flesh, our fallen human nature. As we do this, we are fulfilling the closing words of 1 Corinthians 6:20: "Therefore glorify God in your body, and in your spirit, which are God's." The glory of the Lord filled both the tabernacle and the temple as God's servants were obedient to God's plans and pattern.

In like manner, we can glorify God in our body as we are obedient to God's plan, that is, His will for us. Do you remember the mystery of God's will—"Christ in you, the hope of glory"? The more there is of Christ, the more there will be of His glory. The purpose of the Christian life is to build a house for God, so that He may have all the glory and we may have all the blessing.

9

CONSIDER YOUR WAYS

WE MAY NOW RESUME the story of the heroes who failed. We
saw in chapter 7 what wonderful people they were, and how
they responded to the call of God. We saw that they left their
homes and their security to make the dangerous journey to
Jerusalem for one special purpose, to build a house for God.
We realized that they had no other reason for making such
a trip. God had called them out with no other challenge but
to build a house for God.

Then in chapter 8 we saw the tremendous significance of
the house of God. It was not just another building, it was to
reestablish the centrality of God. They knew that when the
building was finished, God would make His presence real.
Just as in the case of the tabernacle and the temple, they
could count on God's presence—His name, His eyes, His
heart. God's promise would guarantee God's presence and
God's presence would guarantee God's power. For seventy
years there had been no temple and the reality of the Lord
was missing from their Jewish culture. They had sung sad
songs and lived on memories, but now was an opportunity to
know God in a new and living way.

But we also know that they failed. We met them first in
Haggai 1:6, in all the misery of failure: no crops, no clothing,
no money. They who had once known wealth and luxury
were now destitute. Let us find out how this came about.
Remember, the Bible tells us to examine their failure, so that
we can be helped, warned, and challenged by their mistakes.

We will turn back to Ezra 3 and trace their foosteps and their failure. We see in verses 1 and 2 that the leaders of the new group were Joshua, the priest and spiritual leader, and Zerubbabel, the prince and political leader. These two men gathered all the people together in the seventh month and built the altar of the God of Israel. Verse 6 tells how they began "to offer burnt offerings unto the Lord. But the foundation of the temple of the LORD was not yet laid."

Verse 8 begins with these remarkable words: "Now in the second year of their coming unto the house of God at Jerusalem . . . began . . . they to set forward the work of the house of the LORD." It was two full years before they made a start on the job they had come to do. We can only assume that these two years were spent on clearing the site and making it ready for the great task ahead.

Think of the wild, unchecked growth of vegetation covering the whole area. Think of the way the great army of Nebuchadnezzar had toppled over every wall in every building, and had so destroyed the city and its surrounding walls that the main problem was knowing where to begin. And all they had were bare hands with which to clear away the vegetation and to move the tumbled stones and heaped-up piles of rubble. Their hands had once been soft and well cared for; now they knew the hardness of daily toil. Their backs and limbs suffered much as they sweated in the heat of the day.

The remainder of chapter 3 tells that they laid the foundation of the house of the Lord. It is a pathetic story to read, recapturing the scene as it took place. Here were these heroes with their fervent enthusiasm seeking to repeat what happened when Solomon had finished the first temple. You remember from 2 Chronicles 5:13 the glorious choir in white linen, the orchestra, the 120 trumpets, and how they sang, "For He is good: for his mercy endureth for ever." It was at that moment that the glory of the Lord had filled Solomon's temple hundreds of years before.

Now these brave people tried to imitate that tremendous performance. Verse 10 tells, "they set the priests in their apparel with trumpets and the Levites . . . with cymbals, to praise the LORD." Verse 11 tells us what they sang: "Because he is good, for his mercy endureth for ever." The same words as were sung in Solomon's day. Here they were, standing in the broken shambles of what had once been the glorious city of God, singing and praising the Lord with such sincerity— and all they were doing was laying the foundation stones!

Solomon had done this only at the end of the building program; but these heroes were so eager to anticipate the presence of the Lord that they did it at the very beginning. What abounding enthusiasm! The emotions aroused by the occasion are well described in verses 12 and 13. Here we learn that "many of the priests and Levites and chief of the fathers, who were ancient men, that had seen the first house, when the foundation of this house was laid before their eyes, wept with a loud voice; and many shouted aloud for joy: so that the people could not discern the noise of the shout of joy from the noise of the weeping of the people . . . the noise was heard afar off."

This was, without doubt, a wonderful start to the glorious task of building a house for God. But then they ran into trouble, real trouble. There were other people living in the area, non-Jews, people who are called the adversaries. These people come with the request, "Let us build with you: for we seek your God" (4:2).

To these the Jewish leaders replied, "Ye have nothing to do with us to build an house unto our God; but we ourselves together will build unto the LORD God of Israel" (v. 3).

We see the reaction of the adversaries: "Then the people of the land weakened the hands of the people of Judah, and troubled them in building" (v. 4). They even went so far as to hire counsellors who wrote a letter to the new King Artaxerxes. In this letter they told a pack of lies. They

described the Jews as being well on their way with the task
of building the walls of the city. Then they suggested that
the king search in the records of his country and discover
what a "rebellious and bad city" Jerusalem had been. It had
caused much trouble in past years and would no doubt renew
that same trouble if rebuilt.

The king searched his records and found "that this city of
old time hath made insurrection against kings, and that rebellion and sedition have been made therein" (v. 19). He then
commanded, "that this city be not builded." The adversaries,
as soon as they received the king's letter, rushed round and
"made them to cease by force and power. Then ceased the
work of the house of God which is at Jerusalem."

What a blow that must have been to these heroes; a lying
letter and an ambiguous reply brought everything to a halt.
And nothing was done about it for fifteen years. Just imagine,
for fifteen years with half-built walls the house of God stood
empty and open to the skies. As time went by, people lost
their fervor and vision and turned to other things. They
accepted the failure and did nothing about it.

Then a new era opened in their history: "Then the prophets, Haggai the prophet, and Zechariah the son of Iddo,
prophesied unto the Jews that were in Judah and Jerusalem
in the name of the God of Israel, even unto them" (Ezra
5:1). These two men changed the whole situation.

Now we can turn to Haggai and see what brought about
such a needed dramatic change. The first chapter of Haggai
opens with a tremendous challenge from God. Haggai was
possibly only a boy when he came with the group seventeen
years before. Now he was moved and stirred to the depths of
his being. For fifteen years he had seen the house of God
lying open, unfinished, uncared for. He exploded, "Thus
speaketh the LORD of hosts saying, This people say, The time
is not come, the time the LORD's house should be built"
(Hag 1:2).

What had happened to that glorious enthusiasm and devotion to God? The tears and the shouts of joy of fifteen years before were lost in the indifference of a careless people. When Haggai had asked when they intended to continue building, he had received the same answer everywhere: "The time is not come, the time that the LORD's house should be built." In other words, "There are more important things to do just now. Of course we intend to build the temple, but let us get on with what we are doing now!" It is hard to believe that these were the same people. They had set out with a burning zeal for one purpose only, and now they have lost their vision.

Haggai returns to the attack: "Is it time for you, O ye, to dwell in your cieled houses, and this house lie waste?" (1:4). Here he points to their own houses, all finished and beautiful, and then he directs their attention to the half-built house of God.

In England we have some wonderful ruins of castles. I can see one from my home, the castle from which came the last wife of King Henry VIII. It is falling down as the years go by, but even so, it has served its purpose. People lived there and worked out the business of daily life. For years it was occupied; now it is a ruin, a graceful ruin that has fulfilled its purpose. All such ruins have a satisfied appearance; history has used them and abused them, and now it is all over.

But this was not so with the half-built temple in Jerusalem. Such abandoned buildings, wherever they are, have a sad, unloved, unwanted appearance. They have never fulfilled a purpose! So it was in Jerusalem. There was the lonely, forgotten, half-built temple of God. The whole thing was an insult to God and a shame to the people; but no one cared, they were seeking to live with an unfinished witness. Strangers passing by might say, "What is that strange place?" and the Jews would reply, "Oh, that is the house of God." What a mockery.

The whole purpose of the house of God was to bring God

into the picture: His name, His eyes, His heart. But because they had given up, they had no sense of the presence or power of God. They were in Canaan without God, in Jerusalem without Jehovah! The whole thing was a travesty of the truth.

At this point the Holy Spirit comes to us and challenges us as to our way of life. Is Christ real in our experience? Are we seeking day by day to recognize His presence and allow Him to control our lives as we make a new behavior pattern? Being saved by the death of Christ is one thing; being daily saved from fear and failure by His life indwelling us is something else. Always remember that God did not save us to be failures. As we recognize the indwelling Christ we are demonstrating a finished temple. Indwelt by His Spirit we can go on to know the glory and the grace of His presence and power.

But as we go on to live the Christian life in our own strength, we become like these people in Haggai's day. We believe in the indwelling Christ, just as they believed in the house of the Lord. But we say, "The time has not come to make Christ real in my life" repeating almost word for word the feeble, defeated words of verse 2.

Then it was that God spoke the words we have already heard: "Consider your ways. Ye have sown much, and bring in little" (vv. 5-6). God challenged them to take a long, hard look at their lives: "Ye looked for much and, lo, it came to little; and when ye brought it home, I did blow upon it. Why? Saith the LORD of hosts. Because of mine house that is waste, and ye run every man unto his own house." God told them that all the failures in crops and shortage in production had come through His will. God had been trying to speak to them, to get them to wake up to their real problem.

They had reasoned that when they could make a success of their business, they would build the house of the Lord. God told them it was the other way around; if they would build the house for Him, then and only then would they know blessing through His presence and His power.

Can you see yourself in this story? Are you seeking to get on in life, to become a real success so that you can then settle down and live a useful life for God—after you have done all that you have planned?

Then God moved in with a new approach. We will see, in a moment, the absolute and amazing love of God stepping out in new areas of blessing. God challenged them once more to consider their ways and then He added: "Go up to the mountain, and bring wood, and build the house; and I will take pleasure in it, and I will be glorified, saith the LORD" (vv. 7,8).

Here was a positive challenge, some way in which they could demonstrate their response to God. God told them to stop everything they were doing and give their full time and attention to the temple: go, bring, build. This is the actual turning point in this story. They have had a challenge, now what will they do? On their immediate decision rests the whole future of their life in Jerusalem. God sometimes brings us to such moments: do we really mean business with God, or are we content to go on playing church?

Here I want you to see the response of the people. The old burning desire for God was not lost but was just buried beneath the dust of doubt and failure. A tremendous response came. Zerubbabel and Joshua and all the people "obeyed the voice of the LORD their God . . . and the people did fear before the LORD" (v. 12). They became the people we met earlier in their story. They had been the heroes who failed; now they became the heroes who found their faith once more.

What a joy this was to the heart of God! He had been yearning over them all those fifteen wasted years, loving them and waiting for them to turn once more to His ways. See now the most amazing part of this story. God did something for them He had never done before. In the days of Moses and Solomon, God had waited until the structure was completed before He filled the tabernacle and temple with His glory. But now see what happened: "Then spake Haggai the LORD's messenger in the LORD's message unto the people, saying, I am with you, saith the LORD."

They who had been so discouraged, so cut off from God by their own willful failure, now were assured of the presence of God. God was with them, even though the building was not finished. All that had changed was their attitude to God. No one had as yet been to the mountain to bring wood and build, because there had not been time. But the heart of God could wait no longer. He saw them, He loved them, and He pitied them.

And so God did a new thing. He became real to them even in the midst of their failure. This is what God can do for us. He can become real to us, vitally and wonderfully real, in the midst of all our failure, if we will do what they did. If, by a change of attitude, we are prepared to recognize ourselves as the house of God, to yield our lives to the indwelling Christ, to be willing to make new behavior patterns to His glory, then we too will know the wonder of those same words: "I am with you alway, even unto the end of the world."

10

CONSIDER MY WAYS

HAGGAI, CHAPTER 1, shows a confrontation with God. The heroes had failed. Their one great mission had been abandoned. They had settled down to accept failure as normal and the result was poverty in every aspect of life.

Then came Haggai with his searching cry: "Consider your ways." This was a challenge to stop and really take stock of the life they were then living. The people dared to listen to God, and slowly but surely the message came through. They had their priorities wrong. They were quite ready to build a house for God after they had managed to cope with the pressing problems all around them. God's call told them to reverse the order: build the house for God and then trust Him to work out the hopeless issues of daily living.

The turning point of the story, we saw, was when the people obeyed and made the tremendous decision to leave everything and to build the house for God. We saw the response of God to their humble repentant hearts: He did something new. God did not wait until the house was completed, as in the days of Moses and Solomon. He sent out the thrilling news: "I am with you."

We saw how the heart of God had been yearning over His people, waiting only to see them respond to His command. Now in this section we will look at chapter 2 of Haggai and see what happened when God almost could have been saying, "Consider My ways; now see what I will do!"

Chapter 2 begins with the people recommencing the building. For over fifteen years nothing had been done and now they reported for duty once more. The first thing God did for them was to restore their confidence, to build up their spirit of enthusiasm. It was one matter, under tremendous emotion, for them to say they would build once more; it was quite another matter to get to the actual physical effort involved. Enthusiasm is one thing; fulfillment is another.

And so God read their thoughts and realized the way their minds were turning. They were comparing the magnificence of Solomon's temple with this pitiful seventeen-year-old abandoned building. There was no comparison. Some of the very old men who had seen the temple of Solomon were talking about it to the young men. As is usual with older men, they talked about the good old days, of the gold that was everywhere on the temple, that shone and glistened in the sunshine, in their days.

God spoke: "Who is left among you that saw this house in her first glory? and how do you see it now? is it not in your eyes in comparison of it as nothing?" (2:3). But then He went on to remind them of the most important thing in the temple. "Yet now be strong, O Zerubbabel . . . O Joshua . . . all ye people of the land, saith the LORD, and work: for I am with you, saith the LORD of hosts" (v. 4). The Lord was actually with them, there and then. This was greater than Solomon's temple had experienced while it was in building. In verse 5 God also adds, "My spirit remaineth among you: fear ye not." Not only was God there, He was going to remain there—so, away with fear.

Then Haggai started to prophesy. Filled with God's Spirit, he told of the future of the house of the Lord: "I will shake all nations, and the desire of all nations shall come: and I will fill this house with glory, saith the LORD of hosts" (v. 7). Some commentators see "the desire of all nations" as pointing ahead to the Lord Himself: He will come, and God will fill this house with glory. What a tremendous thought!

God answered, as it were, the people who were talking about the gold of Solomon's temple and of how poor this new temple would be in comparison. "The silver is mine, and the gold is mine, saith the LORD of hosts" (v. 8). God already had the gold; what He wanted now was the glad hearts of His people.

God then gave a tremendous promise: "The glory of this latter house shall be greater than of the former, saith the LORD of hosts" (v. 9). How could such a poor forgotten building excel the glory of the golden temple? But that was the promise of God.

And then God added one more precious promise: "And in this place will I give peace, saith the LORD of hosts" (v. 9). They had known no peace for years, only poverty and frustration. But here was God saying to consider His ways.

You will recall that the people had been trying to straighten out the social and economic situation before they got down to the business of making God real. You will remember that God told them they had their values wrong: first make God real, then the rest will follow.

Now see how the Lord demonstrated this in His promises. First He spoke, as we have just seen, concerning the temple. Then He went on, as we shall now see, to deal with the trouble. Three times the Lord urged the people, "And now, I pray you, consider from this day and upward" (v. 15), "Consider now from this day and upward. . . . Consider it" (v. 18). What they had to consider was the failure in the agricultural program. Everything had gone wrong. Then they had to consider that from that very day, "before a stone was laid upon a stone in the temple of the Lord," God was going to bless them.

Just imagine how these words would encourage the people in their poverty: "Is the seed yet in the barn? yea, as yet the vine, and the fig tree, and the pomegranate, and the olive tree, hath not brought forth: from this day will I bless you" (verse 19). God was dealing with the practical matters of life.

In many areas where the church is today, there is an increasing emphasis on what is called the social gospel. I see it especially as I travel to countries where the standard of living is low, and the people are struggling to make a living. I hear the same emphasis that was made by the people in Haggai's day: "Sure, we will preach the gospel and bring the people to the Lord, but first of all, let us get the economic situation under control. Let us go ahead and organize new methods of farming, let us teach them so that they can have a better standard of living. Then when they are economically sound and have managed to cope with their problems, we will preach the gospel and tell them about their need of Jesus." This sounds humane and is in line with modern activist thinking, but does it work? Do people come to God when they are at peace and have found a measure of satisfaction? Does outward security and sufficiency make for virile Christian living?

History points to just the opposite. Jesus said in Luke 5:31, "They that are whole need not a physician; but they that are sick." The scriptural order is seen in Haggai. First give God His rightful place, and then the solutions to needs will follow. Notice especially there was no long time lapse between the two events of obedience and blessing. There is no reason why the two should not happen almost simultaneously, so long as right and true relationships are established with the Lord.

Remember also why we are using this story of "the heroes who failed. We are seeing it especially in relation to believers, those who really trust the Lord, and in the matter of rebellion and independence from God. So far these people have given us an illustration of what happens when true Christians fail to make Jesus real in their lives. When they fail to apply the pattern and truth of the temple in their own lives, then they too are left without the presence and power of God. They can be engaged in a perfectly legitimate work, as were the people in Jerusalem. Building a home is no sin; developing a farm or ranch is no sin. What they were doing was not sin as such, but it was a substitute for what they were called out to do.

What we all need to realize, as believers, is the one purpose for which we were called. The whole Christian life is an increasing experience of involvement with Christ. First we meet Him at the cross, and by His death He saves us from our sins and assures us of a home in heaven. All this comes to us through an involvement with the saving death of Christ.

Then, having been saved by His death, we go on to a developing involvement with His saving life. As I yield my life to Him to use as He will, and as I recognize His indwelling presence, seeing my whole being as the temple of the Holy Spirit, then my Saviour is able to use me for His glory and in His service. There are many Christians whom the Lord cannot use because He cannot get His hands on them. They are busy running their own lives, working out their own particular brand of independence. It sometimes takes nothing less than a shock experience to get them to consider their ways.

In the previous chapter we saw Ezra mention the two men who were used to call the people back to God. One was Haggai, whose story we have just read. The other was Zechariah, whose book follows Haggai's.

This Zechariah was a remarkable prophet. He gave some exciting prophecies concerning our Lord. In Zechariah 9:9 we read the story of Jesus' entry into Jerusalem on a donkey. In chapter 11 comes the prophecy of the thirty pieces of silver being paid for the price of Jesus, later flung down on the floor of the house of the Lord, and finally used to purchase the potter's field (vv. 12, 13). One prophecy has yet to be fulfilled: "And his feet shall stand in that day upon the mount of Olives" (14:4). This speaks of His coming again.

I mention the above so that we can see the caliber of this man who joined Haggai in stirring the hearts of the people in Jerusalem.

His main work was to encourage the people when they had made a start. Let us see how God used him to tell the people, "Consider my ways."

The people began to build "in the four and twentieth day of the sixth month, in the second year of Darius the King" (Hag 1:15). Notice that God's Word pinpoints the very day in history when the heroes began again. Zechariah 1:1 says, "In the eighth month, in the second year of Darius, came the word of the Lord unto Zechariah." So Zechariah began prophesying two months after the rebuilding commenced.

His main emphasis was the reality of the presence of God and also the great love of God for these struggling people who had given up so much for God, only to fail. We read, "Therefore thus saith the LORD; I am returned to Jerusalem with mercies: my house shall be built in it, saith the LORD of hosts" (v. 1:16). Notice the assurance of God's presence and the assurance of completion. This time building will not cease, leaving the temple to stand empty again.

Then comes a lovely phrase which has passed into our English language as a figure of speech: "For he that toucheth you toucheth the apple of his eye" (v. 2:8). How precious they were to God.

Following this we read in verses 10 and 11, "Sing and rejoice, O daughter of Zion: for, lo, I come, and I will dwell in the midst of thee, saith the LORD . . . I will dwell in the midst of thee." As the temple was in the center of their city, and God was in His temple, so He was in the midst.

Zechariah had some special words for Zerubbabel, the prince. These statements have long since passed into the vocabulary of many Christians. We will recognize the challenge: "Then he answered and spake unto me, saying, This is the word of the Lord unto Zerubbabel, saying, Not by might, nor by power, but by my spirit, saith the Lord of hosts" (v. 4:6). We like to use these words in our own connection, but notice that they especially applied to this prince as he tried to motivate and lead the people.

See these encouraging words for the leader: "The hands of Zerubbabel have laid the foundation of this house; his hands shall finish it; and thou shalt know that the Lord of hosts hath sent me unto you. For who hath despised the day of small things?" (vv. 4:9, 10). That last phrase, *the day of small things*, is in current English usage, but see how it would especially apply to the building they were doing. Some of the people present might despise it; the heathen around would certainly despise it; but God did not despise it!

Zechariah presented a beautiful, complete picture of what God had for His people. His prophecy pointed to a coming day as well, but we can see it especially in reference to these heroes who failed.

> Thus saith the Lord; I am returned unto Zion, and will dwell in the midst of Jerusalem: and Jerusalem shall be called a city of truth; and the mountain of the Lord of hosts the holy mountain.
>
> Thus saith the Lord of hosts; There shall yet old men and old women dwell in the streets of Jerusalem, and every man with his staff in his hand for every age.
>
> And the streets of the city shall be full of boys and girls playing in the streets thereof.
>
> Thus saith the Lord of hosts; If it be marvellous in the eyes of the remnant of this people in these days, should it also be marvellous in mine eyes? saith the Lord of hosts.
>
> Thus saith the Lord of hosts; Behold, I will save my people from the east country, and from the west country.
>
> And I will bring them, and they shall dwell in the midst of Jerusalem: and they shall be my people, and I will be their God, in truth and in righteousness (Zec 8:3-8).

Just think, all this love and all this blessing was in the heart of God, waiting for these people to turn from their independent ways of failure. For fifteen years God waited to pour it out on His people. It was theirs through all the wasted empty years, but it only came true when they came back to dependence upon God, when they came back and began a new behavior pattern based not on their own efforts, but on God's presence and God's power.

Certainly it cost them "blood, toil, tears and sweat," but the One in control was God, and blessing was inevitable.

And God says the same to us today; there is so much love, power, and blessing all ready for us to enjoy, if we, too, will come and admit our failure, make Jesus real in our hearts, and start a new behavior pattern.

11

REBELLION: TAKING LESS THAN
GOD'S BEST

IN EVERY HUMAN HEART there is a longing for completeness, a yearning to do, to have, and to be. This desire for fulfilment is inborn, and it shows itself in so many ways: the longing for fulfilment through marriage and family, through education, through wealth, or through art. Whatever country I visit, regardless of race or culture, I see this craving for completeness increasing.

Much of the unrest among students and young people is a searching for fulfilment, a rejection of what is seen around them, a reaching out for something finer and more satisfying. We need to know this and to recognize it when we see it.

The sudden rise of the drug subculture is a demonstration of this very thing. It presents a way of escape from the surrounding failure, but it can never satisfy the inner longings of the human heart. It may appease for a while, but the price of appeasement increases as each experience develops. It takes more and more to produce less and less, and unless the victim realizes this and gets out in time, it becomes the way of no return. Just remember the figures we quoted in chapter 2: 100,000 young people died in the United States from an overdose of drugs in the five years ending in 1969, two and one-half times the United States' Vietnam war deaths for the same period.

They tried to find an experience of completeness in this

world through drugs; all they found was the completeness of death.

We need to realize that the desire for completeness is not a sin. The method used may become sinful and evil, but the desire is inherent; it was put there by God. God had a reason for making us this way, as we can see in Colossians 2:9, 10: "For in him [Christ] dwelleth all the fulness of the Godhead bodily. And ye are complete in him, which is the head of all principality and power."

God made us with a built-in sense of incompleteness. He wants us to reach out for fulfilment, but He has so ordained that we can only be complete in Christ. All the good desires we have for the fulfilment in family, material things, and lovely experiences are excellent. They all play their part, but they can never completely satisfy. The divorcee who seeks completeness through another partner, the eager businessman who seeks his completeness through money and power, the artist who seeks it in music, writing, or graphic expression: all are doomed to failure.

We are spiritual beings, not just two-legged animals, and our completeness can only come in and through the Holy Spirit.

What we need to realize is that we can only be complete in a complete Christ. We have seen already what it is that God offers: a twofold experience of Christ in our lives.

We can receive Him as the One Who died for us on the cross. By His saving death we receive forgiveness of sin and a home in heaven. We can then go on to receive Him by His saving life, as He indwells us by His Holy Spirit. This latter way is a daily experience of making Christ real in our hearts through the new behavior pattern.

When we receive all that God gives, then we can go on to grow day by day toward an increasing sense of completeness. Not that we will ever arrive or be perfect in this world. Even Paul said as much in his letter to the Philippians: "Not as though I had already attained, either were already perfect: but I follow after" (3:12).

It is this sense of taking all that God gives, of knowing the fulness of Christ, that produces the quality of life God intended us to live. If I only take half of what God gives, then I can only enjoy half a Christian experience. If all I take is the wonder and glory of the saving death of Christ, then my sins are forgiven and I have a home in heaven, but I have no capacity to live here and now in the world around me.

The saving death of Christ does not qualify me to live, it qualifies me to die and go to heaven as a forgiven sinner. It is the indwelling saving life of Christ that qualifies me to live now. Jesus said in John 14:19, "Because I live, ye shall live also."

The tragedy is that so many Christians have taken less than God's best. They became involved at the cross with the death of Christ, but they have not gone on to be involved with the life of Christ.

It is this aspect of rebellion that we are considering in this present chapter. The rebellion of taking less than God's best, of being so dependent at the cross, but of choosing to live our own lives—good, bad, or indifferent—with no daily dependence on the indwelling Christ.

We are going to study this subject of taking less than God's best by looking at a fascinating story as it unfolds in the Old Testament.

We have the authority of 1 Corinthians 10:1-12 for following this story. The Holy Spirit in this chapter tells us to examine the story of the experiences of the children of Israel as they moved out of Egypt into Canaan. Verses 6 and 11 tell us to note the mistakes that they made, the sins they committed. We are to see in what ways they failed God and came short of His plan for them. The reason for doing this is not just to condemn them, but to see ourselves in their mistakes. Verse 6 says, "Now these things were our examples." Verses

11 and 12 say, "Now all these things happened unto them for ensamples [or types of ourselves]: and they are written for our admonition [our warning] . . . Wherefore let him that thinketh he standeth take heed lest he fall." Notice the special warning in the closing phrase for any who are self-confident and so feel no need of such a challenge.

We can pick up the story in Deuteronomy, chapter 1. This whole book is a remarkable study. It begins with these words: "These be the words which Moses spake unto all Israel on this side Jordan in the wilderness." The entire book is a postmortem on the failure of Israel to go into Canaan, plus laws and words of instruction for when they eventually do make it.

Notice who spoke it and wrote it—Moses. Notice where it was compiled—in the wilderness, on "this side Jordan." This latter phrase means they were near the Jordan but still in the wilderness. It was also written at the close of the forty years' wandering in the same wilderness. The last chapter was added by another writer. It includes the details of Moses' death. Thus, Deuteronomy begins with a post-mortem and ends with a death.

We can pick out from Moses' account key words and phrases that tell us what really was God's best.

The first key is found in verses 2 and 3: " (There are eleven days' journey from Horeb by the way of Mount Seir unto Kadesh-barnea.) And it came to pass in the fortieth year." A simple statement, but what an awful indictment. They could have made the journey to Kadesh-barnea in eleven days. This place was the point of entry into Canaan. They could have been in Canaan in less than three weeks, but it took them forty years before they finally made it. What a terrible tragedy that was, stuck in a wilderness for forty years when all the time they could have been in Canaan.

Further evidence is found in chapter 6: "And when thy son asketh thee in time to come, saying, What mean the testimonies and the statutes" (6:20). Here follow instructions for a father in days to come. When his son asked for information about the journey, the father had to tell this son, "We were Pharaoh's bondmen in Egypt; and the LORD brought us out of Egypt with a mighty hand . . . he brought us out from thence, that he might bring us in, to give us the land which he sware unto our fathers" (6:21, 23). Notice what God's plan was, He was going to bring them out of Egypt and straight into Canaan—two weeks later! The wilderness was not part of God's plan. It was the rebellion of the people that put them there. They condemned themselves to forty years' wilderness wandering.

This same thought is brought out in chapter 12: "Ye shall not do after all the things that we do here this day, every man whatsoever is right in his own eyes. For ye are not as yet come to the rest and the inheritance, which the LORD your God giveth you" (12:8, 9).

See that description of independence in verse 8: every man doing what is right in his own eyes. Notice it is not doing wrong, but doing right in his own eyes. That is what put them in the wilderness and that is what kept them in the wilderness—going their own way. Notice the tenses in verse 9; God was giving them a rest and an inheritance in Canaan. It had been theirs for forty years, but they had not found the rest and the inheritance. See the implications of this; there is no rest or inheritance in the wilderness.

We were told in 1 Corinthians 10 that the experiences of these people were types of our experience. Let us see how this is so today. The story of the whole plan of redemption from Egypt is a perfect illustration and type of our redemption through Christ. They were in bondage in Egypt; we are in bondage to sin. They were redeemed by the blood of a lamb at the Passover. 1 Corinthians 5:7 says, "For even Christ our passover is sacrificed for us."

God's plan for them, as we have seen, was to bring them

out of Egypt and right on into Canaan. The wilderness experience was no part of God's salvation, although God used it to teach them many lessons.

In like manner, God's plan for the Christian today is two-fold: out of Egypt and into Canaan. Egypt, as we saw, is the type of bondage from which we were redeemed by the blood of the Lamb. But what is Canaan? If we go by the hymns we sing, then Canaan is heaven, "On Canaan's happy shore." But this is definitely not so in the teaching of the Bible. Canaan was a place where there was much fighting; there is no fighting in heaven. No, Canaan does not represent heaven; it stands for the other half of God's salvation.

All along we have seen the twofold gift of God in Christ, a complete salvation in a complete Christ: His saving death and His saving life. His saving death is the wonder of His sacrifice at the cross, "Christ our Passover, sacrificed for us." His saving life is all that He can be to me day by day as I continue to make the new behavior pattern.

God's plan for the believer is that he should come to know Christ as his Saviour at the cross. Then, being indwelt by the risen victorious Christ in the person of His Holy Spirit, he should go on straight away to know the saving life of Christ. This twofold experience of Christ should follow on immediately, the one after the other.

But as it happened with the children of Israel long ago— forty years in a wilderness of their own provision—so it happens with many believers. Of course they come to know Christ at the cross, otherwise they would not be true believers. But then, like the people in Deuteronomy 12:8, 9, they go on to do whatever is right in their own eyes, and as a result, they have no rest and they enjoy no inheritance. Ephesians 1:11, speaking of Christ, says, "In whom also we have obtained an inheritance." Further on in verse 14, speaking of the Holy Spirit, we read, "Which is the earnest [the present proof] of our inheritance."

The risen victorious Christ indwelling me is my inheritance here and now. As I learn to rest in Him, trust in Him, commit to Him day by day, then I begin to enjoy my inheritance and I move into the spiritual Canaan of God's provision. As the days go by, I have battles to fight and enemies to face, but with Christ real in my life, I can begin to experience victory.

If I take only half of God's glorious gift, if I know only the saving death of Christ, then I have to do my best to live the Christian life. I start doing what is right in my own eyes, facing life in my own strength, and as a result, I condemn myself to my own particular wilderness where there is no rest and no inheritance.

Some Christians never get out of the wilderness! Oh yes, they are saved, and they will go to heaven when they die, but they never experience that wonderful quality of Christian living where Christ becomes a daily reality. Others spend years in the wilderness until God, in His mercy, shows them the wonder of the saving life of Christ.

Why is it that some do, and some don't? A lot of failure is due to ignorance, not to willful disobedience. They never hear the full story of the complete Christ. They only know, "Come to Jesus and get your sins forgiven!" Thank God for the glory of Calvary, but thank God more for the glory of the Christ who rose again and who comes to indwell us by His Holy Spirit.

Some hear it, but somehow it fails to make sense to them. With some people a year or two pass before what they have heard begins to make sense in their experiences. Until the believer appropriates all that God gives, he is guilty of taking less than God's best, and inasmuch as he takes less than God's best then he is walking in independence, which is rebellion.

This story of the final entry into Canaan becomes amazingly interesting when we follow the hopes and desires of one particular group of people. This special story begins in Numbers 32. By the time we reach this chapter, the forty years of wandering are nearly over. All those who came out of Egypt were dead, as God had ordained, except Moses and Joshua and Caleb. This was a new generation facing up to life. They had known nothing but the life in the wilderness, all its deadness, all its limitations.

As they moved on in their journeys out of the real wilderness into the fringe of the wilderness, they found the area becoming more fertile by comparison. They had conquered the people who lived in that area and taken possession of their cattle. They were reaching small towns and seeing houses. All this to them would seem tremendous in comparison with the empty loneliness of the wilderness: real permanent homes, not tents.

So it was there came a desire into the hearts of the children of Reuben and of Gad. Their leaders came to Moses with a proposition. They explained that they had "a very great multitude of cattle." They also said they had been examining the area into which they were moving, the fringe wilderness, and they felt it was an area very suitable for raising livestock. "Wherefore, said they, if we have found grace in thy sight, let this land be given unto thy servants for a possession, and bring us not over Jordan."

They had never seen Canaan. They had no idea how wonderfully fertile their promised land was. They were tired of wandering, and the fringe of the wilderness looked so exciting after the dreary deserts they had seen in other places. They did not want their inheritance. They were quite happy to settle for less than God's best. And so they pleaded with Moses, "bring us not over Jordan."

Moses' first reaction was one of anger. He assumed that they wanted to drop out of the march into Canaan, "Shall your brethren go to war, and shall ye sit here?" Instead of twelve tribes fighting the enemy in Canaan, there would only be ten. Moses was thinking of the battles ahead and of how every soldier would be needed to gain the victory.

Then these eager leaders of Reuben and Gad came up with a brilliant suggestion. Verse sixteen tells:

> And they came near unto him, and said, We will build sheepfolds, here for our cattle, and cities for our little ones;
>
> But we ourselves will go ready armed before the children of Israel, until we have brought them unto their place: and our little ones shall dwell in the fenced cities because of the inhabitants of the land.
>
> We will not return unto our homes, until the children of Israel have inherited every man his inheritance.
>
> For we will not inherit with them on yonder side Jordan, or forward; because our inheritance is fallen to us on this side Jordan eastward (Num 32:16-19).

To Moses, this was a most attractive deal. There were 40,000 armed men aged twenty and over in these two tribes. These could be a tremendous help without women or children to distract them. They could be a fast-moving, mobile attack force, or they could go before and clear the way for the main body following in the rear.

But see what it meant to the women of the two tribes staying in the wilderness. There were no men for leadership or protection. Their children would grow up unprotected from both the physical and the moral dangers all around them. The people still living in that area were pagans who worshipped evil sensuous gods. There were rites and ceremonies full of debauchery all connected with this worship, and their children would be left exposed to all this lustful culture.

No priests stayed to teach the Word of the Lord, for they all went over Jordan; no tabernacle for worship, nothing to hold them true to the Lord, but everything to take them away from the pure ways of Jehovah God.

Teenagers are the same all the world over. Just imagine

how these desert wanderers would be attracted to the life
and ways of the "big cities," however small they were.

But such was the burning desire of these men of Reuben
and Gad that they were willing to risk their families and
their children. They spoke of having an inheritance in the
wilderness, but this was never part of the plan of God. Canaan
was their glorious inheritance, not this improved wilderness
situation.

We are told in 1 Corinthians 10 to be warned by these
mistakes. Christians too can do as did Reuben and Gad. The
men will sacrifice their children in order to carry out their
own special plans. God has a wonderful plan for their life,
if only they will move into Canaan and make Christ real day
by day, yield to Him, and make Him Lord of their lives.
Then the whole family will be blessed as they stay together
in the things of the Lord. One of the curses of America today
is the broken, divided home. This is what happened with
these men in our story. They chose to break up their homes
to satisfy their own ambitions which were so much less than
God's best. In all this they were moving out in independence.

Moses was at fault also. It wasn't often that he made a
decision without consulting the Lord, but this time he
couldn't resist the offer of a special advance army. Without
stopping to consider or pray about it, he readily accepted this
offer and clinched the deal before they had time to change
their minds. Thus we read in verse 33 that Moses gave two
kingdoms with their land and cities to the tribes of Gad and
Reuben, and also the half-tribe of Manasseh. Notice that half
another tribe had joined the group, cashing in on the good
deal!

See these words in verse 33: "Moses gave unto them." We
are going to find that phrase coming again and again. God
never gave it to them; Moses did. God gave them Canaan
forty years before. It was theirs all the time they wasted the
years in the wilderness. God never saved us to be failures;

He gave us Christ. The miserable wildernesses in which we grind out our daily lives come through our own desires to take less than God's best.

The following verses tell of a strange situation. They list the towns and cities that were occupied by these two and a half tribes, but verse 38 tells that they changed the names of the places. The places remained the same, with all the heathen potential for sin and sorrow, but the names were changed to sound better when they spoke about them. Sin is sin whatever we call it. Using new and pseudoscientific words to describe lust and sin and moral wickedness may change the sound of our conversation, but it doesn't alter the evil of our behavior.

Our story now moves on to Joshua, chapter 1. Here we read that Moses died and Joshua took over the leadership of the nation. We read in verse 2 God's first words to Joshua: "Moses my servant is dead; now therefore arise, go over this Jordan, thou and all this people, unto the land which I do give to them." See the words of the Lord: "thou and *all* this people." God wanted twelve tribes in Canaan, not nine and a half. This was the command of the Lord.

Now see how Joshua handled this situation. In verse 11 he commanded the people to prepare to pass over in three days, "to go in to possess the land, which the LORD your God giveth you to possess it." Finally he spoke to the two and a half tribes: "Your wives, your little ones, and your cattle, shall remain in the land which Moses gave you on this side Jordan; but ye shall pass before your brethren armed" (Jos 1:14).

This was not the plan of God. Joshua was simply perpetuating the failure of Moses. Notice the comparison, "the land which the Lord your God giveth you" and "the land which Moses gave you." The whole thing was so stupid, so foolish; they were condemning their wives and children to a moral destruction, but they thought they knew best. Learn how one leader's mistake can be perpetuated until it eventually destroys the whole plan. This can happen in any movement, great or small. Because Moses had said it, it had to be so, even though it was in contradiction to the Word of the Lord.

And so the wives and children stayed in the wilderness to fail, and the men went off into Canaan to conquer.

We meet these men again in Joshua, chapter 22. The events recorded here take place five years after the crossing of Jordan. Joshua called together the men of the two and a half tribes and said, "Ye have kept all that Moses the servant of the Lord commanded you . . . ye have not left your brethren these many days . . . and now the Lord your God hath given rest unto your brethren, as he promised them: therefore now return ye, and get you unto your tents, and unto the land of your possession, which Moses the servant of the Lord gave you on the other side Jordan."

See the implications of this. These men had not been home for over five years. They had left their wives and children in the awful place of temptation with no men to control or guide. Boys had grown up without ever seeing a man of their own race. Every man was in Canaan; the only men in their area were the heathen who dwelt in the land! See again those same words, "the land which Moses gave you." Joshua said their brethren had found rest in their inheritance, thus God had fulfilled His promise, but there was no rest for these men, because there was no inheritance in the land which Moses gave them.

We see a very challenging thought in verse 19. Here Joshua is bidding farewell to these men before they make their final departure. He urged them: "If the land of your possession be unclean, then pass ye over unto the land of the possession of the Lord, wherein the Lord's tabernacle dwelleth, and take possession among us."

He gave them a second chance. Now they had seen all the beauty and wonder of Canaan; they could compare their

possessions in the wilderness with "the land of the possession
of the LORD." If they changed their minds there was still
room for them in Canaan, just as God had planned. Notice
that Joshua said, "if the land of your possession be unclean."
It was unclean in every way: there was no tabernacle, no
priests, no presence of God.

The question was, would they stay in the wilderness, or
would they see their mistake and move into Canaan, to find
their rest and their inheritance? The answer was, they stayed
in the wilderness. We may well ask, why on earth stay in the
wilderness when they had seen God's best? The answer is
found in the words of our Lord in John 3:19: "This is the
condemnation, that light is come into the world, and men
loved darkness rather than light, because their deeds were
evil."

The families who had dwelt in those pagan places for five
years were rooted there. The teenagers the men had left
behind were young adults when they returned. They were
strangers to their fathers. Instead of the fathers drawing their
children on to Canaan, the children drew their fathers back
to the wilderness. We know this is true because we have one
more scripture to read in 1 Chronicles 5:18-26. These verses
tell what wonderful fighters came from "the sons of Reuben,
and the Gadites, and half the tribe of Manasseh." They were
wonderful fighters because that had been their chosen task.
But then verse 25 tells, not of their strength, but of their
weakness: "And they transgressed against the God of their
fathers, and went a whoring after the gods of the people of
the land, whom God destroyed before them."

"And the God of Israel stirred up the spirit of Pul king
of Assyria and . . . Tilgath-pilneser king of Assyria, and he
carried them away, even the Reubenites, and the Gadites,
and the half tribe of Manasseh . . . unto this day." See those
words, "unto this day"; they mark the end of those foolish
people. Time and again they had a chance to find rest and

inheritance in Canaan, but no, they wanted their own way, less than God's best. Out of Egypt, yes; into Canaan, no! And so, they lost everything they possessed; and all the time they could have enjoyed everything that God possessed.

And these verses in 1 Corinthians 10 keep challenging us; is this you? Have you made the same mistake? Out of Egypt, yes; into Canaan, no! Have you taken all the blessings of the saving death of Christ: sins forgiven, a home in heaven? Now, have you gone that one stage further; have you taken all the blessings of the saving life of Christ? Is He real, day by day, as you fight your battles, or have you settled for less than God's best?

12

REBELLION: THE FORGOTTEN
NAME

IN THE EPISCOPAL CHURCH service there is an act of worship
called the General Confession. This is said by the minister
and the people as they confess to God their failures and their
sins. It begins, "Almighty and most merciful Father; We
have erred, and strayed from Thy ways like lost sheep. We
have followed too much the devices and desires of our own
hearts. We have offended against Thy Holy laws. We have
left undone those things which we ought to have done; And
we have done those things which we ought not to have done;
And there is no health in us."

How true to say there is no health in us, for two basic
reasons: we have left undone those things which we ought to
have done, and we have done those things which we ought
not to have done. In this chapter we are going to consider
one of the most pathetic stories in the Old Testament. It is
about a young man who possessed everything but enjoyed
nothing. But before we come to his story, let us look in
Matthew, chapter 1, and find the mystery of the forgotten
name.

The Christmas story begins in verse 18, a well-known and
much-loved account. In verse 21 the angel is speaking to
Joseph and says, "she shall bring forth a son, and thou shalt
call his name Jesus: for he shall save his people from their
sins." The end of verse 25 tells us that Joseph was obedient
to the command. This blessed name Jesus is the one that

fills all our hearts with joy and worship. "How sweet the name of Jesus sounds in a believer's ear." It tells us of forgiveness and peace and a home in heaven.

But then in verses 22 and 23 we read, "Now all this was done, that it might be fulfilled which was spoken of the Lord by the prophet, saying, Behold, a virgin shall be with child, and shall bring forth a son, and they shall call his name Emmanuel, which being interpreted is, God with us." Notice here is another name, Emmanuel. This verse says, "They shall call his name Emmanuel."

Verse 21 said, "Thou shalt call his name Jesus," and that is exactly what Joseph did. Verse 23 says, "They shall call his name Emmanuel, God with us," and the tragedy is that this is the forgotten name; they do not call His name Emmanuel. We know Him by the lovely name Jesus, but not much reference is made to the other wonderful name.

The last words of Matthew's Gospel are spoken by the Lord, and He says, "And, lo, I am with you alway, even unto the end of the world." Can you see the name Emmanuel there: "I am with you alway"?

Matthew's gospel begins and ends with this precious name and yet, to many believers, it carries little significance. We all rejoice in the name Jesus, but so many miss the added blessing of Emmanuel.

Just consider these two names for a moment. The name Jesus tells us what He did: He saved His people from their sins. The name Emmanuel tells us who He is: God with us. What He did, and who He is.

Jesus is the name connected with the saving death of Christ, that He bore our sins in His body on the tree. Emmanuel is the name connected with the saving life of Christ, that He ever lives in my heart to be my strength day by day.

Jesus is the name which tells that He saved me from my sins; Emmanuel, that He saves me from my self. Remember your biggest problem is not your past sins, but your present self. You are your greatest problem, your greatest enemy. The more I know of the implications of the forgotten name, the more I will be able to live here and now.

Jesus is His name as the sin-bearer. Emmanuel is His name as the burden-bearer, day by day. There will be some of you reading these words who are carrying burdens God never intended you to bear. Your sins are gone because of the wonder of Jesus. But your burdens remain because you have never come to know the unfolding glory of His presence day by day.

We began this chapter by recalling that "there is no health in us," because we have left undone those things which we ought to have done, and we have done those things which we ought not to have done. We have a positive and a negative behavior problem.

Let us look into the Old Testament and see the sad story of a young man who had the same problem, and what God did about it.

We read in Matthew 1:22, "now all this was done that it might be fulfilled which was spoken of the Lord by the prophet, saying," and then we saw the reference to Emmanuel. Most Christians know that these words are a quotation from Isaiah 7:14, "There the Lord himself shall give you a sign; Behold, a virgin shall conceive, and bear a son, and shall call his name Immanuel." But do you know to whom these words were first spoken? Who was the first person to hear these glorious words foretelling the virgin birth of our Lord? If you did not know, you might reason thus: such glorious words must have been first given to a person whose life was worthy of such a blessing, someone holy, faithful to God, a great saint. But you would be wrong; he was one of the greatest rebels recorded in the Old Testament, a man full of problems, full of failure, and yet a man most religious in all his ways.

We can begin his story in 2 Chronicles 28. This is how we

meet him: "Ahaz was twenty years old when he began to reign, and he reigned sixteen years in Jerusalem; but he did not that which was right in the sight of the LORD." He was king upon God's throne, God's man in God's place, when he was only twenty. He was dead and buried when he was thirty-six. Put in the context of today in the United States, he would be a college man, a radical, rebelling and demonstrating in his own misguided, confused way. Sometimes we get the idea that all the kings and prophets in the Old Testament were old men, feeble and decrepit. But this is not so; time and again we meet young men in these positions behaving just like some young college people behave today. The Old Testament has many radicals recorded in its pages and their stories make relevant reading in today's world scene. Ahaz was one of the most consistent rebels in the book.

His basic problem was that, like Israel today, he was surrounded by enemies. On all his borders there were guerrilla bands making incursions into his kingdom. He was in desperate trouble; he needed all the help he could get. But, the amazing thing was that he would not turn to God and seek help from the Lord of hosts. He was the king with all power, he could do exactly what he wished and desired, but he could not solve the problem of the enemy attacks.

Verses 3 and 4 in this chapter tell of some of the attempts he made to reach the gods in his land: "Moreover he burnt incense in the valley of the son of Hinnom, and burnt his children in the fire, after the abominations of the heathen whom the LORD had cast out before the children of Israel. He sacrificed also and burnt incense in the high places, and on the hills, and under every green tree."

These verses record his pagan practice to enlist the help of idols and false gods. See that it says, "and burnt his children in the fire." This hideous act only serves to show how sincere he was in his practice of religion. There was a vile god called Molech, who demanded human sacrifice. Little babies were thrown into the fire of sacrifice, their little lives given to pay the god to assist the worshiper. This passage says he burnt his children in the fire; more than one of his own babies died in the flames of Molech, seeking to buy help against the enemy.

The whole chapter is a build up of tragedy as Ahaz went his own way, frantically seeking help. Verse 18 gives a list of places captured by the Philistines and it goes on to say why, "For the LORD brought Judah low because of Ahaz king of Israel; for he made Judah naked and transgressed sore against the LORD." God was trying to get through to this young rebel, to bring him to his knees in confession and supplication.

Verses 20 to 22 tell that he tried to buy help from the king of Assyria. Ahaz took gold out of the house of the Lord, Solomon's glorious temple, and from his own purse and from the money of his princes. This he sent to the heathen king, but the Scripture records that he wasn't helped by this king. Verse 22 says, "and in the time of his distress did he trespass yet more against the LORD: this is that King Ahaz." That last phrase is a bitter cry, almost as if the writer is spitting out the words, "this is *that* King Ahaz."

Verse 23 records, "For he sacrificed unto the gods of Damascus, which smote him: and he said, Because the gods of the kings of Syria help them, therefore will I sacrifice to them, that they may help me. But they were the ruin of him, and of all Israel."

It seems unbelievable that he could be so stupid, turning to pagan gods, and all the time he lived next door to the house of the Lord. As we shall see in a moment, God was longing to help him, waiting for this young man to realize his hopeless inability to "go it alone." His rebellion was ruining his country, destroying his own family; but still he persisted, trying to find his own way out of the desperate situation.

The Bible tells us to measure ourselves against such stupidity, and the tragedy is that there are Christians who will also sacrifice anything to get their own way. We, too, find it hard to humble ourselves and come to the Lord, throwing ourselves on His mercy and trusting only in His power.

More about the man Ahaz is told in 2 Kings, chapter 16, especially one unusual incident. The chapter begins as before by listing his age, his death, his constant pagan worship, his ever-increasing difficulties. Then in verse 10 we read of a visit he made to Damascus to meet the king of Assyria, the one to whom he paid so much money. While he was there, he saw an altar. There was something about this altar that really fascinated him. It was a pagan altar of sacrifice and he conceived the idea that if he had an altar like that, he would really have power and success. So he ordered one of his men, so qualified, to draw, "the fashion of the altar, and the pattern of it, according to all the workmanship thereof." Then he sent this design to Urijah, the high priest, at the temple in Jerusalem. He instructed Urijah to make an exact copy of this altar, so that when he returned he could try something new in his religious experiences.

We read what happened when he returned. The first thing he did was to offer four different kinds of offerings on his altar, as recorded in verse 13. But then he had a problem: what should he do with the other means of worship put there by King Solomon, at the direct order and plan of God, when it was first built?

God had established the pattern and the plan for worship in His holy temple. As the worshiper entered the wide, open courtyard he was faced, first, with the brazen altar. This was a magnificent structure on which the worshipper offered his sin offering as he made his approach to God. The priest who made the offering then went toward the building called the holy place. But before he entered, he cleansed himself at a large water container called the laver. This was a huge bowl resting on lion-shaped supports. God's order was threefold: confession and sacrifice for sin, then the cleansing, then the entrance to worship.

But now Ahaz had brought his new pagan altar into the courtyard of God's holy house. It is almost unbelievable to read what he next commanded. Verse 14 says "And he brought also the brasen altar, which was before the LORD, from the forefront of the house, from between the altar and the house of the LORD, and put it on the north side of the altar." They moved God's altar to one side and left Ahaz's pagan altar at the entrance of the courtyard.

Then he had the laver of cleansing taken down and moved to one side, so that, when he had finished his remodelling, all he had was his own new, exciting pagan altar alone before the holy house of the Lord. He revised his theology—and perished. We can read in verse 15 the orders he gave concerning worship to God. He listed the offerings to be made, but he made no mention of a sin offering. There was no offering for sin, no cleansing, as God had ordained, only his own special altar and his own special sacrifice. Ahaz expected the Lord of hosts to come down to his miserable level and accept what Ahaz chose to do. No recognition of sin, no repentance for sin, just an arrogant demonstration of self-will. The end of verse 15 records his added comment concerning the holy brazen altar: "and the brasen altar shall be for me to enquire by." He would ask God questions at the brazen altar. How ridiculous; the brazen altar was a place of confession of sin, not a place of argument or discussion.

And yet God still loved this young man, just as He still loved the two and a half tribes who chose less than God's best. "God desireth not the death of a sinner, but rather that he should turn from his wickedness and live." In just the same way, the Lord gets no joy or glory when His people are crushed and limited by their own foolish failures. He is ever ready to forgive, to love and restore. If we turn to Isaiah, chapter 7, we can see a picture of the heart of God reaching out to this embittered rebel.

As we read the first half of this chapter, we see the humility of God. Ahaz would not turn to God, so God sent Isaiah to speak to him. Verses 1 and 2 tell once more of enemies moving in on Ahaz. "And his heart was moved, and the heart of his people, as the trees of the wood are moved with the wind" (v. 2). A vivid picture of the fear filling his heart.

Isaiah came to Ahaz and said, "Take heed, and be quiet; fear not, neither be fainthearted" (v. 4). He then went on to tell of what God had planned, and ended with these words: "If ye will not believe, surely ye shall not be established" (v. 9). Then we read two glorious verses. It almost seems improper to have them there; it is not right that the Lord should have to stoop so low. Ahaz would not come to God, and he would not listen to Isaiah; so we read, "Moreover the LORD spake again unto Ahaz, saying, ask thee a sign of the LORD thy God; ask it either in the depth, or in the height above" (vv. 10-11).

The Lord Himself spoke to Ahaz. See how He said, "Ask thee a sign of the Lord thy God"; see the words *thy God*. The Lord had not given up Ahaz, even though Ahaz would have no dealings with God. I find this a most moving passage, God Almighty stooping to speak in love to a rebel who had consistently shunned the presence of the Lord. Who but a loving heavenly Father would be so tender and patient.

Notice that the Lord encouraged Ahaz to ask for a sign either from earth or from heaven. Surely Ahaz would respond to such an overture of love from his God. See what his answer was: "But Ahaz said, I will not ask, neither will I tempt the Lord" (v. 12). Almost as if he had flung back in the face of a loving heavenly Father His offer of love, and mercy and help. How could a man be so wretchedly ungrateful? To think of all the failure in the life of Ahaz, and here was the one clear chance of success. He had been seeking peace all his reign, but when it was within his grasp, he pushed it away in bitter rebellion.

No wonder Isaiah came back with words almost full of disgust: "Hear ye now, O house of David; Is it a small thing for you to weary men, but will ye weary my God also?" (v. 13).

Then came this glorious promise from the heart of God. With the smoldering bitterness of Ahaz still there, the whole atmosphere tense with this build up of ingratitude, we read this precious jewel of God's own devising: "Therefore the Lord himself shall give you a sign; Behold a virgin shall conceive, and bear a son, and shall call his name Immanuel." Who would have dreamed of finding such a verse in such a context!

But now see the tremendous importance of the verse in this pitiful setting. Ahaz is the typical picture of a self-willed, obstinate, ungrateful rebel. He is the example of a man seeking peace, constantly overwhelmed with problems, at his wits' end to know where to turn. To all such the Word of God comes ringing down the years; there is an answer. God will send His son, born of a virgin, to be Immanuel, "God with us."

Thank God for Jesus who came to save the sinner; but now, thank God for Emmanuel who comes to save the saint from himself, his fears, his helplessness.

All that Ahaz needed he could have found in the Lord of hosts, if only he would come, but he turned away, to perish. All that you and I need is found in Emmanuel, the risen, victorious Christ who indwells us by His Holy Spirit. Isaiah's word still has meaning: "If ye will not believe, surely ye shall not be established."

"They shall call his name Emmanuel, God with us." Do you know Him by this name?

13

LORDSHIP: THE ANSWER TO REBELLION

IN THE LAST FEW CHAPTERS of this book, we have been looking at pictures of God's people in rebellion. We have seen the absolute failure of such an attitude, and the Lord has been speaking to our hearts, challenging us to see ourselves mirrored in their behavior.

In this chapter I want us to look at a man who is a picture of just the opposite behavior. This man is almost an unknown in our Bible stories; he is so overshadowed by the others around him. But before we turn to find him, look with me in Luke, chapter 2, to where we see, once more, the Christmas story.

Do you know who were the first preachers of the gospel during the earthly lifetime of our Lord Jesus? It always surprises some people to find that the gospel was being proclaimed within minutes of the birth of the Lord Jesus. Verse 9 begins the story of the angels and their visit to the shepherds. Verses 10 and 11 record the first gospel message ever preached during the life of Christ here on this earth: "And the angel said unto them, Fear not: for, behold, I bring you good tidings of great joy, which shall be to all people. For unto you is born this day in the city of David a Saviour, which is Christ the Lord."

This was the message preached, and now look in verse 14 and see what this message was intended to produce here on earth: "Glory to God in the highest, and on earth peace, good will toward men." A twofold message was to bring a three-fold result. But when we compare the words of the angels with the world around us, we see a tremendous difference. We see no glory to God, no peace on earth, and certainly no good will among men. Sadly, if we compare the words of the angels with the lives of many Christians, we still find no glory to God, no peace in their hearts, and an absence of love and goodwill to others.

Yet the reason for this failure is not hard to find. The angels brought a twofold message which was to have a three-fold result. Many believers have responded to only one part of the angelic message, which is why there is no fulfillment in their hearts. The angels' message said, "For unto you is born this day in the city of David a Saviour, which is Christ the Lord." They spoke of a Saviour who is also Lord. I find this lack of response to Christ's lordship is one of the greatest sources of weakness and failure in many Christians lives, both young and old.

Every Christian appreciates Jesus as Saviour. It is so satis-fying to know sins are forgiven and be assured of a home in heaven. It brings a warm sense of security in a world so full of uncertainty. But such a limited response will never bring the glory, the peace, and the goodwill. The threefold result can only be realized when the twofold message is fully responded to, and Jesus becomes not only Saviour but Lord.

Why is there this natural hesitancy to hold back from making Jesus Lord of our lives? I see it in every walk of life, pastors, missionaries, church officers, teachers; all of us are ready to call Him Saviour, but calling Him Lord, in the real meaning, is another thing. Oh yes, many people address Him as Lord. I often hear beautiful prayers full of love to Christ. During such prayers I hear the phrase "Dear Lord Jesus" said with much affection and obvious sincerity. It sounds good; however, the word *Lord* is not a term of affection, but a term of ownership.

In Luke 6:46 Jesus said, "And why call ye me, Lord, Lord, and do not the things which I say?" The one test of submission to lordship is obedience. The idea comes from the lord/slave relationship. If He is my Lord, then I am His slave. A slave had no rights of his own, no possessions, no will—nothing of his own. He was the property of his master. The Bible teaches that we are not our own, but have been bought with a price. Because He bought us, He owns us. We are His slaves, and He is our Lord. The fact that I am faithful and obedient to my Lord and Saviour does not imply any wonderful spirituality in me; this is normal slave behavior.

It is good to realize who pays the price with relation to these two names. When we call Him Saviour, we are acknowledging that He has saved us. The other side of John 3:16 is 1 John 3:16, for it tells us, "Hereby perceive we the love of God, because he laid down his life for us." God the Son laid down His life for us; Jesus paid it all. That is why we call Him Saviour. It costs us nothing to have Him as our Saviour, because all the price was paid by Him.

When we come to the name *Lord*, it is a different story. If Jesus is to be my Lord, then I am to be His slave. I must give up all that I am and have. I must renounce my rights to my own life. I pay the price of submission to Lordship or I don't, whichever the case may be. Christians freely call Jesus "Saviour"; salvation is God's free gift, and it costs them nothing. Many hold back on yielding to His lordship; it costs too much. God has no bargain basement. The cost of submission to His lordship has not changed since it was first introduced. It cannot be increased, because it takes all that I am and have. It will not be decreased because if Jesus is not Lord of all, then He is not Lord at all.

The name *Saviour* is connected with His saving death; the name *Lord* is connected with His saving life. *Saviour* denotes Him as my Advocate in heaven, the One who pleads His precious blood before the throne of God. *Lord* indicates Him as the One to whom I bring my old broken, failing behavior pattern. As I learn to commit myself to Him step-by-step (as we saw in chapter 5), then He builds a new behavior pattern. As I commit my ways, then He directs my path; but He can only do so when my hands are off my life, and He is Lord.

The sad thing is that so many Christians react to the idea of lordship as if they were going to lose out on living. They feel that when they yield their lives to Christ, it is goodbye to all the joy and peace and delights of life. From then on, it is a grim, slogging, grinding experience. This is far from the truth. When I make Him Lord, then I am finished with rebellion. The end of rebellion means the restoration of fellowship, as we saw in Genesis, chapters 2 and 3. And this is why we were created, to have fellowship with God. I never fulfill the purpose for my being created until I make Him Lord, But when I do fulfill the purpose of my creation, only then does life make sense.

Jesus never *takes* from a person anything that is worthy and honorable. He always *adds* to the life of the believer. His lordship, which costs me everything, adds to my life a totally new dimension in living. If my faith costs me nothing, then it is worth nothing. If it costs me everything, then it is worth everything.

This chapter is entitled "Lordship: the Answer to Rebellion." I want us now to look at that special character who so perfectly demonstrates for us the cost of submitting to His lordship.

I have heard many messages concerning the Christmas story. Messages that refer, of course, to Mary and the baby Jesus, then to the shepherds, the wise men, the angels, the inn that had no room; but rarely have I heard a message about Joseph. And yet the more I have thought about this man, the more I have realized what kind of character he had. Consider for a moment that God had to choose a man who was going to be responsible for raising His own Son. He had the whole of history from which to make this choice. Who would you choose to raise your son, if this was the way it had to be? A rich man could provide for all his needs. A scholar would give him the best education. A king could give him power. God could have chosen anybody, and yet He chose Joseph. This should surely mark this man out as being someone superspecial. No wealth, no educational achievements, no power, no genteel sheltered life; just a pair of hard, calloused hands and the skills of a village carpenter, and yet he was God's own selection.

As we look into Joseph's story, we find that there is not a single word recorded as spoken by him. Much was said and spoken by Mary, but Joseph is the strong, silent man. He is not known for what he said, but only for what he did.

If we select the passages in Matthew's gospel where we meet him, we find a noteworthy set of consistent acts. We meet Joseph in four places, and each time he has a real problem on his hands.

We see in Matthew 1:18-19 that he is battling with one of the biggest problems that could ever face a man. The girl he loves and to whom he is engaged has suddenly become pregnant. The child she is bearing is not his. Now what should he do? By the Jewish law she could suffer a severe punishment, if he wishes to raise the matter. But no, he is courteous and kind enough to consider simply breaking off the engagement. And then we read in verse 20: "But while he thought on these things, behold, the angel of the Lord appeared unto him in a dream." How strange, God spoke to him in a dream.

After the birth of Jesus, Joseph has a problem once more. Herod is on the attack, but "behold, the angel of the Lord appeareth to Joseph in a dream" (v. 2:13). Once more, God met him in a dream. Later he is in Egypt, and again we read, "behold, an angel of the Lord appeareth in a dream to

Joseph" (v. 2:19). Finally, when he is perplexed as to where to go, "notwithstanding, being warned of God in a dream, he turned aside into the parts of Galilee" (v. 22).

Four times he has dealings with God, and each time it is by a dream. We could truly call him Joseph the Dreamer. But notice this: he was God's man, and God chose him for the superb excellence of his character. In each case God told him to follow a certain line of action, and it is thrilling to see his immediate response to the lordship of God. Never once did he question how or why; in each case the Bible gives his response not in words, but in actions. We shall see that after each dream, we find three verbs. The whole story of Joseph is a four-times-repeated incident: the dream, followed by three verbs.

Let us weigh the cost of submission to lordship in the life of Joseph. In the first dream, God told him to marry Mary. What a challenge, to marry a pregnant girl—totally against all his principles and his pride and his culture! To marry a bride who was not a virgin was completely unacceptable. But see what Joseph did: "Then Joseph being raised from sleep did as the angel of the Lord had bidden him, and took unto him his wife" (Mt 1:24). Notice the three verbs: "being raised," "did," "took." Not a word of argument or pleading or resistance, just immediate obedience. He sacrificed his honor.

At the time of the second dream, the wise men had just departed, leaving Mary and Joseph bewildered by the magnificence and glory of their visit. "And when they were departed, behold, the angel of the Lord appeared to Joseph in a dream, saying, Arise and take the young child and his mother, and flee into Egypt" (2:13). Just consider the implications of this demand from God. Here he was being asked to leave his own country, to become a refugee, and to fly to another country. What an ordeal—to leave his own land, God's land, to become a total stranger, going to a foreign country where he did not know the language, and to walk all the way. The natural fear and nervousness against making such a move must have risen up in his heart. But see his response: "When he arose, he took the young child and his mother by night, and departed into Egypt" (2:14). There are the three verbs once more: "he arose," "he took," "he departed." Don't miss those two words *by night*. His obedience was such that he went immediately. How easy to have said, "Let us wait until it is day; now it is dark and dangerous outside," but no, he was God's man any time, all the time.

The third demand came when he was safely settled in Egypt. Being a good carpenter, he would soon find himself in a successful business. He was out of all danger. No one knew who they were. Herod's spies did not reach into Egypt. All was well, and then God called again. God called Joseph to leave his new home, the very first home that he and Mary had established, to return to Israel, to the domination of Rome, to the uncertainty of the future.

Verse 21 shows his immediate obedience in the three verbs: "he arose," "and took," "and came." He left his security and his success—because he was God's obedient man.

In the fourth dream he is faced with a problem of choice. Judaea was the best place to be; it was David's country, where his people belonged. But God had other plans. God wanted him back where he began, back to Nazareth, to the old place where he was well known. And so Joseph is warned once more in a dream, and once more we read the set of three words: "being warned of God, in a dream, he turned aside into the parts of Galilee."

"And he came and dwelt in a city called Nazareth." He turned aside . . . he came . . . and dwelt.

And that is all we have in the Bible concerning God's dealing with and through Joseph. What a man—no rebellion, just a constant obedience to God. This was the man who raised the boy Jesus and gave to Him the example of an obedient servant. There would be much busyness in that home in Nazareth as the years went by, but as long as Joseph was there, God had a man he could trust. What a reward Joseph had for his obedience—he had real family fellowship with the Son of God. For the rest of his life, he walked with God. Even when he died, the boy he raised, the Son of God, was there to comfort him in death.

These are the kind of people God is looking for today. Maybe little nobodies, of no importance in the eyes of this world, but as long as Jesus is both Saviour and Lord of their lives, God can still do His mighty work through their yielded lives.

14

IT DOESN'T WORK

As we come to this last chapter, I am well aware that there will be some of you who have read so far and in your mind there is this kind of reasoning: "Yes, this sounds good, but I've tried this commitment thing before and it didn't work."

I have met this reply in various places. The person had gone through all the motions, believed all the beliefs, and then as time went on, he found something was wrong, somewhere, because it didn't work.

Let me share some final thoughts with you from God's Word. I know it works. I have seen lives changed, wonderfully transformed. I am referring to believers, those to whom God has brought a real sense of living. This could be you; your life could be changed.

Look with me in Jeremiah, chapter 29, and hear God speaking to His people on this same subject of reality in living. Verse 11 begins, "For I know the thoughts that I think toward you, saith the Lord, thoughts of peace, and not of evil, to give you an expected end." Here God is saying that He has a plan for your life. Your way may be confused and cloudy, but God knows His way. It is a way of peace, not of failure, "to give you an expected end." It is real; you can count upon it, expect it. He continues, "Then shall ye call upon me, and ye shall go and pray unto me, and I will hearken unto you. And ye shall seek me, and find me, when ye shall search for me with all your heart. And I will be found of you, saith the Lord" (29:12-14).

God is promising all this blessing—of seeking and finding—on one condition, "when ye shall search for me with all your heart." This is the secret of success—and the explanation for failure—"with all your heart." The key word is *all*. This is basically the only reason for failure in human experience, not seeking God with all the heart.

Now look in Psalm 119, the longest psalm in the Bible. There is one key phrase which occurs six times in these verses. See verse 2: "Blessed are they that keep his testimonies, and that seek him with the whole heart." This verse means exactly what it says; it is not just a group of religious words. It is saying there is blessing for you—soul peace, quiet rest in your heart—on one condition, that you seek the Lord with your whole heart.

Verse 9 is a great challenge to youth. How can I cleanse my whole way from sin and shame and impurity, and keep it clean? Again there comes the same answer: "With my whole heart have I sought thee."

All God's blessings become personal and real when I seek Him with my whole heart.

Let us find out now what this phrase means, "all your heart." First of all, what is your heart? These verses certainly don't refer to the fleshly organ that pumps the blood around your body. Well then, where is it? It is surprising how many Christians do not know where their heart is, or what it is. If you do not know what the heart is, you cannot seek Him with all of what you do not know. This, again, is why there is so much failure. Ignorance is often to blame more than insincerity.

The Bible teaches quite simply and plainly that the heart is the human personality. Your heart is the real you. The heart, or personality, is made up of three separate parts. Any good book on psychology will teach you the same concept. The words may be different, but the meaning is the same.

Man is a trinity, in more ways than one. The three parts

are the emotions, the mind, and the will. It is in this same order that they usually function. See how the Lord Jesus taught this truth in His ministry. Concerning the emotions, He said, "For from within, out of the heart of men, proceed evil thoughts, adulteries, fornications, murders, thefts, covetousness, wickedness, deceit, lasciviousness, an evil eye, blasphemy, pride, foolishness" (Mk 7:21-22). What a horrible list of human abominations—all the evil emotions that stir in the lives of men and women! Notice that the Lord said these came out of the heart.

Likewise He said, "Let not your heart be troubled" (Jn 14:1), linking the emotion of fear with the heart. These verses show us the simple truth that the heart is where the emotions are.

Regarding the mind, Jesus said, "Why think ye evil in your heart?" (Mt 9:4). Likewise, when he was speaking to a group of scribes, He said, "Why reason ye . . . in your hearts?" (Mk 2:8). Thus the heart is also the place where we think, plan, reason, scheme—it is the mind of the man.

There is a beautiful verse in Daniel, chapter 1, concerning the young man Daniel as he faced his future life. Like many young people today, he was at a college, studying hard. He had a scholarship which included everything, even the food. The food offered to him, however, had connections with idol worship. Now Daniel loved the Lord, and he wanted no part with anything that might hurt his love for God. And so we read, "But Daniel purposed in his heart that he would not defile himself with the portion of the king's meat" (Dan 1:8). He exercised his will; he "purposed in his heart." The will is the third part of the human heart. Other passages in the Bible add to this same teaching, that the human heart consists of the emotions, the mind, and the will.

Take this information and put it into focus as we see the first phrases again: "when ye shall search for me with all your heart," "that seek him with the whole heart." We can see right away that there is a depth of meaning which we did not consider before.

There is a natural pattern of thinking which assumes that to seek Him with the whole heart means to be more sincere, to try harder, to really work at it. Some think it means to love the Lord more. This is true in a way, but that is not all that it implies.

We will be helped if we realize that "a whole-heart" involvement is not just a spiritual term. God has created us in such a way that we operate in this whole-heart system whatever we are engaged in. Unless our emotions are stirred by the story we are reading, we will put the book down; it has no interest for us. If the TV program does not grip us emotionally, we change to another channel. If the football game does not move us to excitement, we write it off as a poor game. Likewise, it is right and proper that we should be emotionally moved in our response to the Lord and His love for us. Those who condemn the involvement of the emotions in evangelism cannot justify their remarks; this is the way we are made.

But the danger begins when I imagine that all the Lord wants from me is my love. True, I will love Him, and as I continue to meditate on all His goodness, I will love Him more and more. But that is not my whole heart; that is just a part of my heart.

God promises all these blessings to us if we seek Him with the whole heart. We need to consider this more carefully as we talk of dedicating our lives to Him, committing our way to Him. Our heart relationship will begin, as we have seen, with our hearts going out in love. Our emotions are fully involved. But then we need to use our minds, our reasoning faculties, and start to count the cost. If we love Him, are we prepared to open our lives to Him? Are we prepared to pay the cost of a whole-heart relationship. If this were faced up to more honestly, there would probably not be so many great crisis decisions or emotional demonstrations. On the other hand, those that were made with the involvement of mind and reason would probably be more lasting and sincere, more effective in their work for the Lord.

But loving the Lord and counting the cost are not a whole-heart seeking. There must be the yielding of the will. If God is really going to have all there is of me, then He must have my will. I must be ready and willing for His plan to come into being in my life. Without the giving of my will, the other two parts become just empty words.

We can see this illustrated perfectly in the various steps taken in the marriage of two who love each other. Of course, they begin with the great love they have for each other. That is wonderful, but loving each other does not make them husband and wife. Having realized their desire for marriage, they then need to make full use of the mind. They count the cost, plan the procedure, and work out all the necessary details connected with the marriage and their plans, for living after the wedding. All this is good and necessary if the future marriage is going to be built on a sound economic structure. But all this exciting planning does not make them husband and wife. It draws them closer, binds them more lovingly, but it is not enough to make them husband and wife.

Sending out invitations becomes even more exciting. Receiving presents marks the beginning of the end, but it still does not make them husband and wife. They can have the most beautiful wedding: the music, the flowers, and the gown! All these are parts of the dream, but they are not the reality.

There is a part of the ceremony where all voices are hushed. The minister asks the groom certain questions relating to his love and future care for his bride. Then the man replies, "I will." The minister asks similar questions of the bride, and every one listens to hear her say "I will."

Then, and only then, comes that great moment when the minister says, "I now pronounce you man and wife."

It wasn't enough to love each other, or to count the cost and plan correctly—the emotions were there, the mind was there—last of all there had to be the will. Until the will was yielded, there was still time to back out; but once they had yielded their wills to each other, there was then a whole-heart relationship.

This is what we do in marriage, and it is a picture of what we should do in our yielding to God. If we really mean business and want to see our lives grow in vital living power, this is the only way: "when ye shall search for me with all your heart."

All that has been said and written so far in this book, all the promises and opportunities, can really be yours—if you come with a whole heart.

Maybe now you can see why it didn't work in the past. Would you like to know the living Christ real in your life? Do you want new behavior patterns that become dynamic realities instead of experimental theories? Why don't you come with your whole heart, end the rebellion, find the fellowship, and walk in newness of life?

PRAYER OF THE WHOLE HEART

Heavenly Father, I come with a humble spirit, with a broken and contrite heart. Forgive me that for so long I have only given You part of my heart.

I can begin to see now why my life is failing. Thank You for showing me this failure, thank You even more for showing the answer to my need.

Loving Father, I come now with all my heart. My love is all for You, Lord Jesus—how precious You are. I have counted the cost, and I realize that to lose Your fellowship and power is too much for me to risk. Regardless of how it works out, I want Your plan for my life.

Last of all, dear Lord, I yield my will. For so long it has been the one barrier to my full life with You. My will has been in rebellion, even though I am a true Christian, because I have kept it for myself. Here and now I say, "Not my will, but Thine be done."

Into Your hands, Lord Jesus, I commit my whole self through the yielding of my whole heart.

Because of who You are, I expect nothing but blessing—for that is Your will for me.

Thank You, my blessed Lord Jesus.

DATE DUE